ML moo.

 before

Increasing Motor Carrier Productivity

Grant M. Davis
John E. Dillard, Jr.

The Praeger Special Studies program—utilizing the most modern and efficient book production techniques and a selective worldwide distribution network—makes available to the academic, government, and business communities significant, timely research in U.S. and international economic, social, and political development.

Increasing Motor Carrier Productivity

An Empirical Analysis

Praeger Publishers New York London

PRAEGER SPECIAL STUDIES IN U.S. ECONOMIC, SOCIAL, AND POLITICAL ISSUES

Library of Congress Cataloging in Publication Data

Davis, Grant Miller.
    Increasing motor carrier productivity.

    (Praeger special studies in U.S. economic, social,
and political issues)
    Bibliography: p.
    1. Transportation, Automotive—Freight—Management.
2. Motor-trucks—Law and legislation—United States.
I. Dillard, John E., 1947-   joint author.
II. Title.
HE5623.D34   1977   658.5'1   77-7821
ISBN 0-03-022641-4

PRAEGER SPECIAL STUDIES
200 Park Avenue, New York, N.Y., 10017, U.S.A.

Published in the United States of America in 1977
by Praeger Publishers,
A Division of Holt, Rinehart and Winston, CBS, Inc.

789   038   987654321

CONTENTS

LIST OF TABLES AND FIGURES

ix

Increasing Motor Carrier Productivity

Increasing aggregate productivity in all sectors of the U.S. economy is an important societal goal, given the presence of "stagflation." In this regard, a significant segment of the contemporary economic dilemma is related to productivity levels. Indeed, stagnant productivity rates can partially explain the divergence between actual and potential gross national product rates. Although productivity levels can be increased in most industries, the problem confronting the domestic trucking industry is inordinate because of certain restrictive covenants pertaining to weight and length requirements.

Relative to productivity, the regulated segment of the trucking industry produced over 21.3 percent of intercity freight ton-miles* during 1975.[1] This segment of the industry is economically significant because of its common carrier responsibilities† and legal obligations to the shipping public.[2] But the industry functions within a unique production constraint: maximum allowable speed limits are 55 mph. In this regard, productivity in the regulated segment can be increased in three fundamental areas. First, higher speed would facilitate intensifying route utilization,‡ but fuel consumption problems negate increasing productivity in this manner. Second, additional output per man-

---

*Although the ton-mile production unit has been criticized as a measure of output because of its lack of heterogeneity, this production unit is better than none.

†Common carriers are required by law to: charge reasonable rates; avoid undue discrimination; proscribe undue preference and prejudice; and provide service to the extent specified in their respective grants from society.

‡A regular-route common carrier, for instance, established regular points for driver exchange based on the combination of 8-hour driving periods and 60- to 70-mph speed limits.

hour represents an important component of factor cost in the industry, but the industry is essentially people-intensive—not capital-intensive.* Inasmuch as the first and second factors appear to be relatively fixed, a third and most pragmatic factor would be increases in weights and lengths. However, a review of existing state statutes reveals heterogeneous weight and length requirements that seriously contribute to reducing or hindering productivity in the industry.

To provide some historical perspective on the problems derived from varying weight and length requirements, it is important to note that the economic philosophy of the motor-carrier size and weight problem was recognized as early as 1920. An executive of the fledgling trucking industry contended that if restrictions on the type of weight of a vehicle utilizing the highway system made the cost of the transportation over the system unduly high, the public was paying that unduly high price in purchasing those commodities. Yet, if motor trucks transporting immoderate loads inordinately damaged the highway surface, the decrease in the cost of transportation owing to the very heavy loads would be more than counterbalanced by the severe impairment to the highway surface; thus, the public would once again be penalized through excessive road repair costs.[3]

The optimum public-policy remedy to this comprehensive problem obviously is to restore an equilibrium between the restrictions imposed on the trucks and on the roads so that the net compensation for the wear on the road and the cost of truck tonnage transportation be reduced to its minimum. This basic conceptual framework was subsequently expanded to encompass additional aspects of the size and weight question, which contributed to the complexity of the issue.†

Although the validity of this particular philosophy toward motor-carrier weights and dimensions has never constituted a specific issue, consensus does not exist on exactly what this intricate balance should be. In fact, during the interval from 1913–56, each state individually interpreted and defined the relationship. Therefore, the historical development and evolution of restrictive covenants for size and weight maximums resulted from a lack of collaboration on the part of the respective states. Subsequent involvement of the federal

---

*Employment in the industry has increased annually for the past 30 years.

†For instance, the advent of the tandem axle raised questions as to load equivalence of single axles; improved technology in tires necessitated extensive research to establish load limits on pavement structures; greater height in vehicles elicited concern over vertical clearance of overhead structures; increased vehicle width generated investigation of pavement lane widths essential to safe accommodation of traffic; and, with the advent of vehicle combinations, a plethora of problems surfaced relating to safety, off-tracking, lateral-space occupancy, performance, and highway alignment requirements for adequate passing-sight distance.

government perpetuated the inequality because of the presence of grandfather clauses* in resulting federal legislation.

During recent years the motor-carrier industry and its allied proponents have cogently and tenaciously endeavored to obtain size and weight increases predicated primarily on increased productivity. In a letter to the Committee on Public Works, John Sweeny indicated that the Department of Transportation continued to believe that, ". . . an increase in permissive vehicle weight and dimension would bring with it gains in the economical use of highway transport."[4] Testifying before the Subcommittee on Roads in the same year regarding legislation designed to increase allowable sizes and weights, William A. Bresnahan, former managing director of the American Trucking Association (ATA), stated:

> The health and pace of our entire economy are directly related to the ability of the highway transportation industry to operate efficiently and economically, using the most modern equipment available to it. This cannot be done unless the present restrictive freeze in the Federal law is eased . . . and the States are given the opportunity to adopt more realistic and more modern standards.[5]

During the subsequent year, Congressman Fred Schwengel of Iowa submitted several questions to the ATA relative to testimony related to H.R. 11870. One particular inquiry specifically requested documentation of the available evidence that an increase in size and weights would automatically provide for more efficient movement of goods commensurate with less cost. The ATA's written response emphasized that because the trucking industry is a high variable cost industry, an important criteria is payload carried for commensurate cost incurred. Expanded size and weight limitations would create a relatively greater payload for the hauling costs involved.[6] Five years later in 1974, during the latest hearings on truck sizes and weights, the situation was the same—a critical need to improve the efficiency of truck transportation, which could optimally be effectuated through larger weights and dimensions.[7] As in previous years, moreover, there was little experimental proof provided to substantiate this significant claim.

These examples are not isolated but are in part indicative of the general lack of empirical evidence on productivity that has plagued the trucking industry in its quest for expanded sizes and weights. Since advocates of change

---

*A grandfather clause usually grants an exemption to firms or individuals that were previously operating under old standards and allows continuation of those standards.

and modification bear the burden of demonstrating the benefits affiliated with any increases, obviously productivity losses ensuing from restrictive covenants in size and weight maximums should be clearly ascertained and measured. This, in turn, would establish a conceptual framework within which productivity losses or gains can be measured and contrasted with highway costs, user costs, social costs, and social benefits.

Contemporary opponents of weight and dimension aggrandizement contend that size and weight increases cause more rapid deterioration of existing highways; require a tremendous expenditure for wider-higher load-rated bridges; threaten the safety of the motorist by reducing the clearance between passing vehicles, decreasing visability, increasing the difficulty in passing, and adding to the hazards of suction, blast, and spray; diminish a truck's braking capability, weight-to-horsepower ratios, coupling devices, tires, and stability; and provide the trucking industry with a competitive economic advantage over other modes of transportation, such as railroads. Nevertheless, the socioeconomic desirability of larger, heavier vehicles cannot be so easily determined, that is, by negative factors alone. The decisive factor is really to what extent a size and/or weight alteration creates a positive effect within the total system, and counterbalances the negative elements.

To determine the economic impact of restrictive covenants in state size and weight limitations upon truck productivity, relevant facts characteristic of the system to which they pertain must, of course, be identified. These would necessarily include a history of restrictive covenants, an enumeration of the current differences in size and weight maximums, the reasons for these differences, and an evaluation of the potential effect of these varying standards on the current performance of the trucking industry. Since it is not possible to make a responsible decision relative to a size and/or weight change without access to both the positive and negative effects of this change, the purpose of this analysis is essentially to provide a model that can measure productivity loss attributable exclusively to restrictive covenants in size and weight maximums, as well as calculate the productivity change generated by any hypothetical weight or dimension standard.

This analysis deviates from previous investigations of motor-vehicle sizes and weights in that a model will be formulated that will possess the capability to determine:

1. Percentage productivity loss due to restrictive covenants in size and weight maximums between a single state and maximum U.S. standards.
2. Percentage productivity loss due to restrictive covenants in size and weight maximums within any multistate-route configuration.
3. Percentage productivity loss due to restrictive covenants in size and weight maximums between a multistate-route configuration and maximum U.S. standards.

4. Percentage productivity change within a single state for any intrastate alteration of a size or weight category.
5. Percentage productivity change for all states for any federal alteration of a size or weight category.

Quantitative information pertinent to the above five areas should theoretically permit a firm to compute the impact of restrictive covenants in size and weight maximums upon carrier revenues and profits, a government unit to calculate the effect on fiscal flows, and state and federal lawmakers to more accurately determine the appropriateness of modifying existing weight and dimension standards at the present time.

SCOPE AND LIMITATIONS

Figure 1.1 depicts the entire range of elements germane to the field of motor-carrier weight and dimension limitations. However, this investigation is necessarily restricted to the narrow path leading to motor freight industry benefits.* Other factors will be introduced only as they relate to the major topic.

The nature of the data required for construction of the simulation model was twofold: first, the size and weight regulations for each state were necessary; and second, vehicle characteristics for any trucks utilized in the analysis were required. Size and weight data were assembled by consulting individual state statutes and where interpretation was required, documents published by the Department of Transportation, the American Association of State Highway and Transportation Officials, and the Western Highway Institute were jointly compared.

With respect to vehicle characteristics, Table 1.1 reveals the codes assigned to the various commercial vehicle types. Each digit represents the number of axles of a vehicle or of one unit of a vehicle combination. A combination symbol, consisting of two or three parts separated by hyphens, indicates a vehicle combination. The power unit is represented in the first digit of a combination symbol. An "S" in the second part of a combination symbol signifies the presence of a semitrailer, with the power unit being a truck-tractor. A digit appearing without an "S" in either the second or third position in a combination symbol represents a full trailer.

---

*The precise path is: legal limits on vehicle weights and dimensions—vehicle characteristics —transport factors—economy of highway freight operation—motor freight industry benefits.

FIGURE 1.1

Influence Flow between Legal Vehicle Limits, Basic Elements, and Benefits and Costs to Highways, Users, and Society

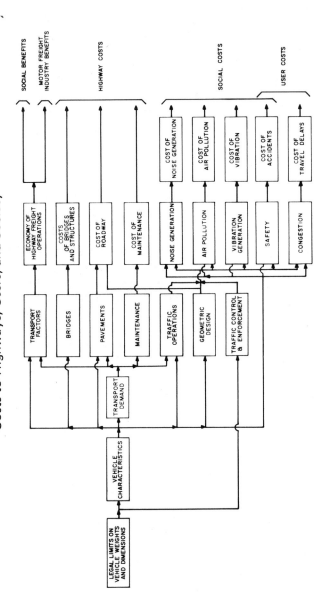

Source: Robert E. Whiteside et al., *Changes in Legal Vehicle Weights and Dimensions: Some Economic Effects on Highways*, National Cooperative Highway Research Program Report 141 (Washington, D.C.: Highway Research Board, National Research Council, National Academy of Sciences, National Academy of Engineering, 1973), p. 14.

TABLE 1.1

Vehicle Axle Code Classifications and Descriptions of Common Commercial Vehicle Types

Axle Code Classification	Description of Truck
2	Two-axle single unit
3	Three-axle single unit
2–S1	Two-axle truck-tractor with one-axle semitrailer
2–S2	Two-axle truck-tractor with two-axle semitrailer
3–S2	Three-axle truck-tractor with two-axle semitrailer
2–1	Two-axle truck with one-axle trailer
2–2	Two-axle truck with two-axle trailer
2–3	Two-axle truck with three-axle trailer
3–2	Three-axle truck with two-axle trailer
2–2	Three-axle truck with three-axle trailer
2–S1–2	Two-axle truck-tractor with one-axle semitrailer and two-axle trailer
2–S2–2	Two-axle truck-tractor with two-axle semitrailer and two-axle trailer
2–S2–3	Two-axle truck-tractor with two-axle semitrailer and three-axle trailer
3–S1–2	Three-axle truck-tractor with one-axle semitrailer and two-axle trailer
3–S2–2	Three-axle truck-tractor with two-axle semitrailer and two-axle trailer
3–S2–3	Three-axle truck-tractor with two-axle semitrailer and three-axle trailer
3–S2–4	Three-axle truck-tractor with two-axle semitrailer and four-axle trailer

Source: U.S., Congress, House, *Maximum Desirable Dimensions and Weights of Vehicles Operated on the Federal-Aid Systems*, 88th Cong., 2d sess., H. Doc. 354, 1964, p. 97; Hoy Stevens, *Line-Haul Trucking Costs in Relation to Vehicle Gross Weights*, Highway Research Board, Bulletin 301 (Washington, D.C.: National Academy of Sciences, National Research Council, 1961), p. 128.

Figure 1.2 illustrates some of the more common commercial vehicle types, as designated by axle code classification, which are engaged in the movement of intercity freight. Eight of these vehicles—the 2-S1, 2-S2, 3-S3, 2-S1-2, 3-S1-2, 3-S2-2, 3-S2-3, and 3-S2-4—were included in the simulation model. The simulation itself represents a deterministic system and should be distinguished from a time-dynamic, stochastic system.

Because of the ambiguity associated with certain terms, the following definitions are used throughout this volume:

Cubic capacity—the inside area of the freight-hauling vehicle.

Cubing out—the complete filling of the cubic capacity prior to reaching any weight restriction, usually gross weight.

Gross vehicle weight—payload plus tare weight.

Kip—1,000 pounds.

Payload—the material contents, commodities, or goods in the truck body that are being hauled and other cargo equipment not included in the tare weight of the vehicle.

Productivity change—alteration of payload and/or cubic capacity.

States—all 50 states plus the District of Columbia.

Tandem axle—two axles spaced at least 40 and not more than 96 inches apart.

Tare weight—the weight of the vehicle or trailer combination without cargo, but prepared for operation on the highway and including full tanks of engine fuel and any equipment regularly carried on the vehicle.

Weighing out—attainment of any weight limitation before the cubic capacity of the vehicle is filled.

Because the intent of this analysis centered on the construction and implementation of a simulation model, no tests of hypotheses were conducted. Instead, an unbiased history of the development of restrictive covenants is presented, together with an enumeration of current size and weight standards. The size and weight data and the previously discussed truck data constituted the data base for the model. Other requisite input data, such as commodity density, route configuration, or hypothetical alteration, were left to the discretion of the reader.

The programming of the model was accomplished in a subset of FORTRAN IV named WATFIV. The analysis utilizing the model was in two parts: a quantitative determination of productivity loss from the viewpoint of the firm and a calculation of productivity change from the standpoint of a government unit. The firm segment simulated vehicle operation in all 108 two-state route combinations for each vehicle type on both highway systems, assuming equivalent ton-mile movement in each state. The government portion of the model employed the Winfrey Study recommendations for federal single- and tandem-axle restrictions on the noninterstate highway system, and simulated the productivity change within all states.

This analysis is divided into five parts. Chapter 2 concentrates on the historical development of various restrictive covenants, and their direct and indirect effects on carrier productivity. In this regard, the interrelationships between motor-fuel taxes, vehicle sizes and weights, and carrier productivity are explained. Chapter 3 is an in-depth review of the contemporary status of vehicle weight and dimension regulation by various government units. Chapter 4 emphasizes the development of a specialized model that permits carriers to

FIGURE 1.2

Commercial Vehicle Types by Axle Code Classification

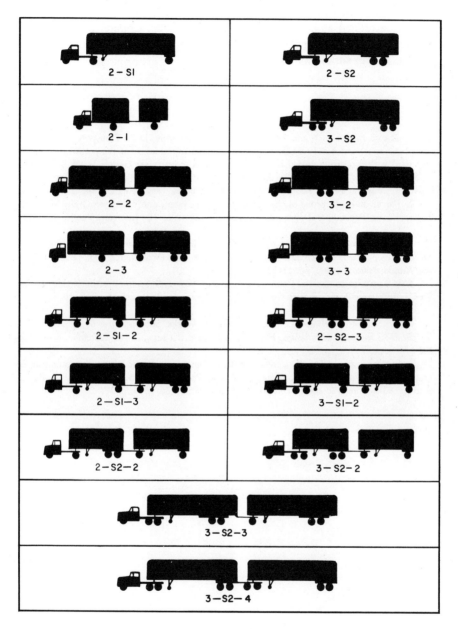

Source: Hoy Stevens, *Line-Haul Trucking Costs in Relation to Vehicle Gross Weights,* Highway Research Board, Bulletin 301 (Washington, D.C.: National Academy of Sciences, National Research Council, 1961), p. 129.

measure the financial impact of restrictive covenants on their productivity and government units to ascertain the impact upon fiscal flows. The chapter contains an extended analysis of the simulation results. Chapter 5 contains the conclusions and public-policy recommendations predicated on historical data and the model simulation.

NOTES

1. *Transportation Facts and Trends,* 11th ed. (Washington, D.C.: Transportation Association of America, October 1975), p. 8. For an in-depth examination of the pertinent problems associated with measuring output in the transportation industry see George W. Wilson, *Essays on Some Unsettled Questions in the Economics of Transportation* (Bloomington, Ind.: Indiana University, Foundation for Economic and Business Studies, 1962), chaps. 1 and 2.

2. For an in-depth probe of the common carrier system and duties see Grant M. Davis, *Transportation Regulation: A Pragmatic Assessment* (Danville, Ill.: Interstate Publishers, 1976), chap. 2.

3. U.S., Department of Transportation, Federal Highway Administration, *Review of Safety and Economic Aspects of Increased Vehicle Sizes and Weights* (Washington, D.C.: Federal Highway Administration, 1969), pp. 11–12.

4. U.S., Congress, Senate, Committee on Public Works, Subcommittee on Roads, *Vehicle Sizes and Weights,* Hearing, 90th Cong., 2d sess., February 19–21 and March 7, 1968, p. 5.

5. Ibid., p. 150.

6. U.S., Congress, House, Committee on Public Works, Subcommittee on Roads, *Vehicle Weight and Dimension Limitations,* Hearing, 91st Cong., 1st sess., July 8–September 4, 1969, p. 208.

7. See, for example, U.S., Congress, Senate, Committee on Public Works, Subcommittee on Transportation, *Transportation and the New Energy Policies (Truck Sizes and Weights),* Part 2, Hearing, 93rd Cong., 2d sess., February 20–21 and March 26, 1974, p. 37.

HISTORICAL DEVELOPMENT OF
RESTRICTIVE COVENANTS AND
THEIR EFFECTS ON PRODUCTIVITY

The motor-fuel tax is unequivocally the most economically significant member of the highway-user tax group, constituting the primary source of revenue for both the construction and maintenance of public highways. The motor-carrier industry, moreover, provides a substantial proportion of these monies annually. An historical review of restrictive covenants contained in state statutory size and weight maximums and in gasoline taxation indicates continued variability for regulations appurtenant to motor-carrier operation. For example, in the size and weight area this lack of uniformity evolved as a direct result of 43 years of separate development by several states and because of the scarcity of coordinated and/or relevant public policy. This observation is plainly evidenced by the pertinent fact that the six states* still maintain the 1913 tire manufacturers' recommendation of 22,400 pounds as a single-axle limitation.

Additional expansion of state size and weight inequality was, until rather recently, stabilized by the Federal-Aid Highway Act of 1956, which established weight and dimension limitations for the interstate system of highways. Although not legally compelled to follow suit, most states at or below the federal requirements incorporated these limits as state maximums. However, those states that maintained higher restrictions were protected by the insertion of a grandfather clause in the 1956 act. This provision, moreover, was to become the quintessence of subsequent polemics, that is, interstate motor-carrier operations and related interests would continue to press for uniformity on productivity grounds and would in turn encounter vigorous opposition on safety grounds.

---

*Maryland, Massachusetts, New Hampshire, New York, Rhode Island, and Vermont.

The basic purpose of this chapter is twofold. First, the various sources and development of restrictive covenants in motor-fuel taxation and in sizes and weights of motor vehicles will be examined. This review will provide the framework for the second purpose of this chapter, which is an examination of intercity carrier productivity. The interrelation of these two purposes is revealed in the economic goal of a viable transportation system, and a financially sound system cannot be hindered by retarding effects.

THE MOTOR-FUEL TAX

Since the colonial period of U.S. history, the development and improvement of basic roads have been critical factors in developing the country's infrastructure. Indeed, the introduction of the privately owned automobile in sufficient quantity during the early 1900s encouraged owners to insist on better highways,[1] but unfortunately did nothing to alleviate the perennial problem of how to finance the improvement.[2] Even though in 1914 the House Ways and Means Committee advocated a two cent per gallon gasoline tax, President Woodrow Wilson ultimately made the first serious suggestion that a tax levied on gasoline consumption could conceivably be used as an additional source of federal revenue. In his annual address to Congress on December 7, 1915, President Wilson stated: "A tax of one cent per gallon on gasoline and naphtha would yield, at the present estimated production, $10,000,000."[3] Although this specific legislative recommendation did not receive serious consideration by the Congress, the suggestion subsequently resulted in the House Revenue Bill of 1918. As a new excise tax, Congress specifically proposed levying a two cent per gallon tax on gasoline for the purpose of providing revenue.[4] But, this provision was not included in the bill's final draft and the gasoline tax issued disappeared for 14 years. The tax ultimately became a statute when the House of Representatives passed the Revenue Bill of 1932 with provisions providing for a two cent per gallon tax on gasoline. This levy was eventually amended to one cent by the Senate, signed by President Herbert Hoover on June 6, 1932, and became effective June 21, 1932.[5]

The total absence of federal legislative activity with respect to a gasoline tax during the 14-year interval between 1918 and 1932 did not hamper state legislation. By 1919, over 7 million automobiles and motor trucks were officially registered in the United States[6] and a new theory of highway financing was emerging. That a gasoline tax would provide an excellent measure of road use was a concept that was expanding for the following reasons: first, the tax would be levied according to mileage; second, nonresidents would contribute toward in-state road expenses; third, heavier and/or faster vehicles, causing greater road impacts, would require additional consumption of gasoline and hence pay higher taxes; and last, areas of high traffic density, which increased road costs, would tend to be characterized by congestion, and frequent stopping and starting, hence more fuel.[7]

These theoretical justifications, together with the necessity for increased building and maintenance of highways, provided the foundation with which Oregon legislature passed a one-cent license tax for motor-vehicle fuel consumption on February 25, 1919.[8] Other states rapidly emulated Oregon's action in adopting this new method of securing revenues for highway purposes, and by 1929 all 48 states plus the District of Columbia were levying this particular tax.[9] Although a majority of states initially introduced a one- or two-cent tax, there were frequent increases that occurred during the 11-year period from 1920–31. These modifications are reflected in Table 2.1. As indicated in Table 2.2, by the time the federal government entered this revenue source in 1932, state tax rates, exclusive of county and city tax rates, already varied between two and seven cents per gallon, with a weighted average rate based on net gallons taxed of 3.60 cents per gallon.[10] As also depicted in Table 2.3, individual state tax rates in subsequent years accelerated so fast that they more than doubled the weighted average tax rate to 7.59 per gallon in 1974.[11]

During the early years, the gasoline tax laws were relatively simple from both a legal and administrative perspective. Legal opposition to the tax developed initially, but a substantial amount of litigation was circumvented by two significant United States Supreme Court decisions, the first rendered in August 1920 and the other ten months later in 1921. In *Askren v. Continental Oil Company,* 252 U.S. 444, the Court ruled that a tax levied upon the sale of gasoline transported in tank cars and the original package into the state and thus sold, exceeded the taxing power of the state because it imposed a burden on interstate commerce in providing for fees in excess of the cost of collection. In a second decision, *Bowman v. Continental Oil Company,* 256 U.S. 642, the Supreme Court declared that a tax assessed on the sale or use of gasoline sold or consumed in the state did not constitute property taxation but was more precisely an excise tax because it operated impartially on all.[12] The significance of these two landmark cases was demonstrated by the fact that throughout the early experience with the gasoline tax they established precedent for nearly all lower court decisions.[13]

By 1929, the gasoline statutes commenced, encountering dual problems: evasions and diversion. Evasion is simply the illegal avoidance of payment of the tax, whereas diversion is allocating tax receipts for nonhighway purposes. An amalgamation of circumstances contributed to the tax difficulties. First, because the original principle underlying the employment of the gasoline tax was to provide financial resources for the upkeep and maintenance of highways, most states developed a system of refunds and/or exemptions from payment of the tax when primary consumption was for nonhighway purposes.[14] A refund, of course, means that the tax is paid but subsequently returned to the consumer; an exemption occurs when the consumer is released

TABLE 2.1
State Gasoline Tax Rates, 1919-31 (cents per gallon)

State	1919	1920	1921	1922	1923	1924
Alabama	—*	—	—	—	2	2
Arizona	—	—	1	1	1–3	3
Arkansas	—	—	1	1	1–3	4
California	—	—	—	—	2	2
Colorado	1–2	1	1	1	2	2
Connecticut	—	—	1	1	1	1
Delaware	—	—	—	—	1	2
Florida	—	—	1	1	1–3	3
Georgia	—	—	1	1	1–3	3
Idaho	—	—	—	—	2	2
Illinois	—	—	—	—	—	—
Indiana	—	—	—	—	2	2
Iowa	—	—	—	—	—	—
Kansas	—	—	—	—	—	—
Kentucky	—	1	1	1	1	1–3
Louisiana	—	—	1	1	1	1–2
Maine	—	—	—	—	1	1
Maryland	—	—	—	1	2	2
Massachusetts	—	—	—	—	—	—
Michigan	—	—	—	—	—	—
Minnesota	—	—	—	—	—	—
Mississippi	—	—	—	1	1	1–3
Missouri	—	—	—	—	—	—
Montana	—	—	1	1	1–2	2
Nebraska	—	—	—	—	—	—
Nevada	—	—	—	—	2	2
New Hampshire	—	—	—	—	1	2
New Jersey	—	—	—	—	—	—
New Mexico	1	2	1	1	1	1
New York	—	—	—	—	—	—
North Carolina	—	—	1	1	1–3	3
North Dakota	1	1	1	1	1	1
Ohio	—	—	—	—	—	—
Oklahoma	—	—	—	—	1	1–2.5
Oregon	1	1	2	2	3	3
Pennsylvania	—	—	1	1	1–2	2
Rhode Island	—	—	—	—	—	—
South Carolina	—	—	—	2	2–3	3
South Dakota	—	—	—	1	1–2	2
Tennessee	—	—	—	—	2	2
Texas	—	—	—	—	1	1
Utah	—	—	—	—	2.5	2.5
Vermont	—	—	—	—	1	1
Virginia	—	—	—	—	3	3
Washington	—	—	1	1	2	2
West Virginia	—	—	—	—	2	2
Wisconsin	—	—	—	—	—	—
Wyoming	—	—	—	—	1	1
District of Columbia	—	—	—	—	—	2
State Average	—	—	—	—	—	—

*Dashes indicate no tax.

Note: The first year in which gasoline taxes were in effect in all states during the entire year was 1930. Weighted averages based on the net gallons taxed are shown.

14

1925	1926	1927	1928	1929	1930	1931
2	2	2–4	4	4	4	4–5
3	3	3–4	4	4	4	4–5
4	4–5	5	5	5	5	5–6
2	2	2–3	3	3	3	3
2	2	2–3	3	3–4	4	4
2	2	2	2	2	2	2
2	2	2	2–3	3	3	3
3–4	4	4–5	5	5–6	6	6–7
3	3–3.5	3.5–4	4	4–6	6	6
2–3	3	4	4	4	4–5	5
—	—	2	—	3	3	3
2–3	3	3	3	3–4	4	4
2	2	2–3	3	3	3	3
2	2	2	2	2–3	3	3
3	5	5	5	5	5	5
2	2	2	2	2–4	4–5	5
1–3	3	3–4	4	4	4	4
2	2	2–4	4	4	4	4
—	—	—	2	2	2–3	3
2	2	2–3	3	3	3	3
2	2	2	2	2–3	3	3
3	4	4	4–5	5	5	5–5.5
2	2	2	2	2	2	2
2	2	3	3	3–5	5	5
2	2	2	2	2–4	4	4
2–4	4	4	4	4	4	4
2	2	2–3	4	4	4	4
—	—	2	2	2	2	2–3
1–3	3	3–5	5	5	5	5
—	—	—	—	2	2	2
3–4	4	4	4	4–5	5	5–6
1	1–2	2	2	3	3	3
2	2	2–3	3	3–4	4	4
2.5–3	3	3	3	3–4	4	4–5
3	3	3	3	4	4	4
2	2	2–3	3	3–4	4–3	3
1	1	1–2	2	2	2	2
3–5	5	5	5	5–6	6	6
2–3	3	3–4	4	4	4	4
2–3	3	3	3	3–5	5	5
1	1	1–3	3–2	4	4	4
2.5–3.5	3.5	3.5	3.5	3.5	3.5	3.5
1–2	2	2–3	3	3–4	4	4
3	3–4.5	4.5	4.5–5	5	5	5
2	2	2	2	2–3	3	3–5
2–3.5	3.5	3.5–4	4	4	4	4
2	2	2	2	2	2	2–4
1–2.5	2.5	2.5–3	3	3–4	4	4
2	2	2	2	2	2	2
—	—	—	—	—	3.35	3.48

Source: U.S., Public Roads Administration, Federal Works Agency, *Highway Statistics, 1946* (Washington, D.C.: Government Printing Office, 1947), p. 8.

15

from tax liability at the time of initial purchase.[15] The expeditious growth of the tax and the system within which it functioned made administration and control of exemptions and refunds increasingly complex. Additionally, the preponderance of higher state tax rates as well as the wide differences of rates among states resulted in evasions of the tax through smuggling and/or refunds and exemptions becoming profitable. Second, whereas gasoline tax proceeds were allocated to nonhighway purposes prior to 1929, available data suggests that the depression furnished the primary impetus, for the diversion of gasoline relief represented a major program in most state legislatures, and the gasoline tax represented a convenient and available source of revenue.[16] (See Table 2.4).

TABLE 2.2

State and Federal Gasoline Tax Rates, 1932
(cents per gallon)

State	Rate	State	Rate
Alabama	5–6	New Hampshire	4
Arizona	5	New Jersey	3
Arkansas	6	New Mexico	5
California	3	New York	2–3
Colorado	4	North Carolina	6
Connecticut	2	North Dakota	3
Delaware	3	Ohio	4
Florida	7	Oklahoma	4
Georgia	6	Oregon	4
Idaho	5	Pennsylvania	3
Illinois	3	Rhode Island	2
Indiana	4	South Carolina	6
Iowa	3	South Dakota	4
Kansas	3	Tennessee	5–6–7
Kentucky	5	Texas	4
Louisiana	5	Utah	3.5–4
Maine	4	Vermont	4
Maryland	4	Virginia	5
Massachusetts	3	Washington	5
Michigan	3	West Virginia	4
Minnesota	3	Wisconsin	4
Mississippi	5.5–6	Wyoming	4
Missouri	2	District of Columbia	2
Montana	5		
Nebraska	4	Federal Tax	1
Nevada	4	State Average	3.60

Source: U.S., Public Roads Administration, Federal Works Agency, *Highway Statistics, 1946* (Washington, D.C.: Government Printing Office, 1947), p. 8.

TABLE 2.3

Weighted Average State Tax Rates, 1946–74

Year	Rate
1946	4.16
1950	4.65
1955	5.35
1960	5.94
1965	6.41
1970	7.01
1971	7.09
1972	7.32
1973	7.53
1974	7.59

Sources: Data for 1946–65 obtained from U.S., Department of Transportation, Federal Highway Administration, Bureau of Public Roads, *Highway Statistics, Summary to 1965* (Washington, D.C.: Government Printing Office, 1967); 1970–73 data extracted from U.S., Department of Transportation, Federal Highway Administration, *Highway Statistics* (Washington, D.C.: Government Printing Office) by individual years; 1974 figure procured from U.S., Department of Transportation, Federal Highway Administration, "News," FWHA 94–75, October 6, 1975.

TABLE 2.4

Diversion of Gasoline Tax Revenues, 1927–37

Year	Amount Diverted in Dollars	Percentage of Total Gasoline Tax Collections
1927	$5,296,921	2.04
1928	7,860,516	2.57
1929	9,260,562	2.14
1930	13,907,302	2.81
1931	18,081,208	3.37
1932	46,289,444	9.02
1933	53,488,050	10.32
1934	89,630,046	15.85
1935	111,246,241	18.03
1936	129,172,000	18.90
1937	130,918,000	17.00

Source: F. G. Crawford, *Motor Fuel Taxation in the United States* (Baltimore: Lord Baltimore Press, 1939), p. 69.

Nevertheless, neither evasion nor diversion of the tax went unnoticed during this period. Many of the principle causes of gasoline tax evasion were eliminated by states that strengthened loopholes, funded additional administrative personnel, and enforced penalties for violation more stringently. By 1946, all but two states had abandoned exemptions as impractical and relied entirely on refunds.[17] Table 2.5 shows a reduction in refunds as a percentage of total tax through the years and indicates the relative stability that refunds have attained during the past two decades. Gasoline tax diversion was accorded national recognition through enactment of the Hayden-Cartwright Act of 1934, which stated in part:

> Since it is unfair and unjust to tax motor-vehicle transportation unless the proceeds of such taxation are applied to the construction, improvement, or maintenance of highways, after June 30, 1935, Federal aid for highway construction shall be extended only to those states that use at least the amounts provided by law on June 18, 1934, for such purposes in each state from state motor vehicle registration fees, licenses, gasoline taxes, and other special taxes on motor-vehicle owners and operators of all kinds of the construction, improvement, and maintenance of highways and administrative expenses in connection therewith, including the retirement of bonds for the payment of which such revenues have been pledged, and for no other purposes . . .[18]

The condemnation effect that most states received as a result of various diversionary practices was twofold. First, it basically caused most state governments to adopt a higher degree of specificity relative to provisions governing the disposition of gasoline tax receipts. Second, several states enacted legislation that specifically prohibited tax revenues from being spent on nonhighway purposes.[19] Data contained in Table 2.6 indicates that funds for nonhighway purposes during recent years have tended to remain a relatively fixed percentage of net collections. Furthermore, the diversion data depicted in Table 2.6 has been confined to a small group of states* that have accounted for 75 to 85 percent of the funds being employed for nonhighway purposes.

In the recent years preceding and following the Second World War, two developments of significant importance to motor-fuel taxation occurred. The first was widespread use of the diesel engine and the second was taxation of gasoline on a use basis.

Albeit anomalies exist in the basic tax structure of the individual states, some ascribable to legislative oversight and others the result of definite purposes, the diesel-fuel tax problem constituted a classic example of a develop-

---

*Depending on the year, anywhere from five to nine states.

TABLE 2.5

Motor-Fuel Tax Refunded for Alleged Nonhighway Use

Year	Amount Refunded in Dollars	Percentage of Total Gasoline Tax Collections
1930	$29,106	5.89
1931	33,392	6.23
1932	35,838	6.99
1933	34,552	6.67
1934	26,968	4.77
1935	31,001	5.03
1936	37,104	5.40
1937	43,210	5.71
1938	46,723	6.09
1939	48,046	5.88
1946	80,250	7.58
1950	140,907	8.49
1955	180,030	7.11
1960	222,458	6.60
1965	203,101	4.53
1970	202,323	3.13
1971	198,745	2.88
1972	199,361	2.63
1973	209,459	2.51
1974	214,284	2.64

Sources: 1930–39 data is from U.S., Public Roads Administration, Federal Works Agency, *Highway Statistics, Summary to 1945,* (Washington, D.C.: Government Printing Office, 1947); subsequent data is collected from U.S. Department of Transportation, Federal Highway Administration, *Highway Statistics* (Washington, D.C.: Government Printing Office) by individual years.

ment not anticipated when original gasoline tax legislation was enacted. As a direct result of this legislative lack of perception, diesel fuel was consumed in numerous states for many years without being subjected to taxation. Today, all of the states except Vermont and Wyoming tax diesel fuel used on public and private highways.[20]

The second problem mentioned above evolved during the early 1940s and focused upon the taxation of interstate trucks. Persons engaged in interstate motor-carrier operations frequently purchased fuel in one state that was consumed in yet another. The net result was that the state in which the fuel was purchased actually benefited from the tax revenue, whereas the state in which the fuel was consumed sustained the unfair burden of providing the highways for other states.[21] The infant trucking industry was cognizant of its financial responsibility in paying a fair share of highway-use taxes and in turn contended

TABLE 2.6

Motor-Fuel Tax Receipts Used for Nonhighway Purposes

Year	Funds Used for Nonhighway Purposes in Dollars	Percentage of Total Gasoline Tax Collection
1955	$90,813	3.59
1960	119,797	3.55
1965	215,199	4.80
1970	314,875	4.87
1971	474,579	6.89
1972	472,637	6.23
1973	463,333	5.56

Note: The amounts shown do not necessarily constitute diversions from highway use requiring a penalty under the terms of the Hayden-Cartwright Act of 1934. Such diversions can be determined only after analysis in light of state laws in force in 1934.

Source: Data is from U.S., Department of Transportation, Federal Highway Administration, *Highway Statistics* (Washington, D.C.: Government Printing Office) by individual years.

that each individual state should receive an equitable proportion of fuel taxes.[22] But, fuel-use taxes have continued through the years to create problems even when general agreements exist. The lack of a uniform and desirable approach for collection of the tax and dealing with various legal difficulties has been detrimental to the states.[23] The motor-carrier industry, as a result of the conflicting and inconsistent state laws, is paying a tax at the time of purchase in one jurisdiction and another tax for consuming the same fuel in yet some other legal jurisdiction. This duplication has, of course, imposed an incremental burden of inequity upon the purely interstate carrier,[24] and, furthermore, has provided the motivational groundwork for third-structure taxes.* A majority of states presently rely on a two-structure system of taxation that incorporates both registration and motor-fuel taxes. But, the dominant tax has remained the motor-fuel tax, which has consistently comprised approximately two-thirds of aggregate highway-user tax collections. The economic significance and magnitude of gasoline taxation is illustrated by data in Table 2.7, which reveals total state highway-user tax information for 1974 and the percent of each burden category supported by trucks. Motor carriers, constituting

---

*It is generally agreed that the user-tax is comprised of the registration fee (tax); motor-fuel tax; and third-structure taxes in three categories: gross receipts taxes, mileage taxes, and fuel surtaxes. The structure of these taxes really refers to the order in which they were introduced, for example, the registration fee is a first-structure tax as it was in operation before the motor-fuel tax (second-structure).

TABLE 2.7

1974 State Highway-User Taxes

	All Motor Vehicles	Trucks	Truck Percent of Total
Registrations	132,852,383	23,462,479	17.7
Registration fees	$3,668,814,000	$1,520,538,000	41.4
Miscellaneous fees	$1,115,698,000	$363,012,000	32.5
Motor-fuel taxes	$8,124,158,000	$2,539,720,000	31.3
Motor-carrier taxes	$215,044,000	$208,852,000	97.1
Total user taxes	$13,123,714,000	$4,632,112,000	35.3

Note: Registrations exclude publicly owned vehicles. Truck registrations include only the power units. Total registrations include motorcycles.

Source: "Truck Taxes by States", 24th annual ed., Department of Research and Transport Economics, American Trucking Associations (n.p., 1975).

17.7 percent of total registration, nevertheless pay 31.3 and 35.3 percent respectively of the total motor-fuel taxes and total user taxes. Virginia in 1942, became the initial state to enforce a comprehensive reporting law, which insured that motor-carrier operators either purchased enough fuel within the state to support their in-state driving or that they paid a tax levy on the equivalent gallonage. All states with the exception of Vermont* presently adhere to Virginia's precedent.[25]

For interstate motor carriers, compliance with state fuel tax laws is of course intricate. The fuel permit identifying the vehicle as belonging to a fleet registered with a state's fuel tax division usually must be renewed annually. Each state, moreover, insists on the periodic submission of cover reports to the fuel tax division that normally must include data such as: (a) total fleet miles traveled in all states; (b) total fuel consumption by the fleet in all states; (c) fleet miles traveled in the taxing states; (d) the computation of fuel consumed in the taxing state; (e) total fuel purchases in the taxing state; and (f) the determination of fuel-tax liability (credit) in the taxing state. The maintenance of detailed carrier records is necessary in order to supply the states items a, b, c, and e. Although typically required, these stipulations are by no means universal to all states. Furthermore, approximately 60 percent of the states compelling fuel reports request that reports be filed on a quarterly basis and the remaining 40 percent require monthly reports. There are a few states, however, in which the prescribed reporting period is left to the discretion of

*Vermont assesses out-of-state trucks a retaliatory trip tax in lieu of fuel tax.

the fuel administrator.* With respect to the annual fuel permit and report-filing regulations, a majority of the states impose fuel-tax bond requirements that guarantee a trucker fuel tax obligations to the state.[26]

VEHICLE SIZES AND WEIGHTS

Government regulation of both sizes and weights of motor vehicles emerged as a fiscal issue at approximately the same time that the Congress was initially debating the need for a gasoline tax.[27] As the gasoline tax served primarily as a source of revenue for maintenance and construction of highways, size and weight legislation was first devised to protect existing highway structures. Initial concern was centered inordinately in three major areas: definition of the relation between load and road; the effects of various static wheel- or axle-load applications by single-unit trucks; and the required density of surfacings to be provided for highway network adumbrating. Although the federal level of government failed to participate in gasoline tax matters until nearly 14 years after the initial state involvement, a 43-year period elapsed between state and federal entry into the sensitive domain of sizes and weights. Needless to say, this substantial time frame fostered and ultimately resulted in an uneven development in the state legislation.

The first weight limitation of an economic significance appeared as the direct result of tire manufacturers' recommendations around 1913. They recommended 800 pounds per inch of width as the maximum economic tire loading. Since 14 inches was the largest prevailing tire width, the resulting 11,200-pound load for the widest tire, or 22,400 pounds for the two wheels of an axle, became a limit that was simply incorporated into many state laws. By 1920, the American Association of State Highway Officials (AASHO) together with the National Automobile Chamber of Commerce, the American Automobile Association, and the Highway Industries Association has proposed a uniform vehicle law that included the 1913 recommendations as a specific limit of axle loading. Although this particular limit was subsequently adopted by many states, little empirical evidence existed to substantiate its relevancy to the supporting capacity of highways.

The year 1920 also marked the beginning of a nationwide program of extensive highway research. The Highway Research Board was organized as a clearing house and forum for all branches of highway engineering; the Bureau of Public Roads initiated tests on different sections of pavement at Arlington, Virginia; experimental roads were constructed by the Illinois State

---

*Florida, Ohio, Oregon, Rhode Island, Wisconsin, and Wyoming.

Highway Department at Bates; and universities in the United States commenced undertaking research and developed into all facets of highway-related activity.[28]

The results of the Bates road tests conducted during 1922–23, together with the impact tests performed by the Bureau of Public Roads, lucidly demonstrated the pertinent relationships existing between pavement and axle-load applications that subsequently provided the essential foundation for AASHO recommendations for maximum weight and dimension limitations proffered in 1932. Table 2.8 illustrates the AASHO weight and dimension recommendation for both 1932 and 1946. However, immediate acceptance of the 1932 proposals by the various state governments was neither comprehensive nor without serious administrative complication. Those states that adopted the AASHO's proposed gross-weight formula, for instance, did not agree on a common value for "C," and variously applied the limits to the spacing of interior groups.

TABLE 2.8

AASHO Weight and Dimension Recommendations for 1932 and 1946

Item	November 17, 1932	April 1, 1946
Width		
present	8.0 feet	8.0 feet
future	—	8.5 feet
Height	12.5 feet	12.5 feet
Length		
single vehicle	35.0 feet	—
single truck	—	35.0 feet
single two-axle bus	—	35.0 feet
single three-axle bus	—	40.0 feet
truck-tractor and semitrailer	35.0 feet	50.0 feet
truck and trailer	45.0 feet	60.0 feet
Permissible loads		
single wheel	8,000 pounds	—
single axle	16,000 pounds	18,000 pounds
tandem axle (under 8-foot spacing)	formula[b]	32,000 pounds
axle groups	formula[b]	table[c]

[a] Dashes indicate no recommendation.

[b] $W = C(L+40)$ with a minimum value of 700 recommended for C, where W = total gross weight, in pounds; C = coefficient to be determined by the individual states; and L = the distance in feet between the first and last axles of a vehicle or combination of vehicles.

[c] Based on the equation $W = 1,025(L+24)-3L^2$

Source: U.S., Congress, Senate, Committee on Interstate and Foreign Commerce, Subcommittee on Domestic Land and Water Transportation, *Study of Domestic Land and Water Transportation,* Hearing, 81st Cong., 2d sess., April 4–July 28, 1950 p. 1,092.

TABLE 2.9

Gross Weight Formulas in Force during 1941

Formula	Enforcing State(s)
$W = 600 (L + 40)$	New Mexico
$W = 650 (L + 40)$	Arkansas, Montana, and Oregon
$W = 670 (L + 40)$	West Virginia
$W = 700 (L + 40)$	Arkansas, Colorado, Georgia, Indiana, Kansas, Oregon, South Carolina, Texas, Utah, and Montana
$W = 750 (L + 40)$	Maryland, Oregon, and Washington
$W = 800 (L + 40)$	California
$W = 1,000 (L + 40)$	West Virginia
$W = 1,330 (L + 40)$	West Virginia
$W = 24,000 + 450 (D)^a$	Iowa
$W = 24,000 + 600 (D)$	New York and Wyoming
$W = 24,000 + 700 (D)$	Indiana
$W = 30,000 + 750 (D)^b$	New York and Ohio

[a] This is equivalent to $W = 450 (L + 533.33)$.

[b] This is equivalent to $W = 750 (L + 40)$.

Source: U.S., Congress, House, *Federal Regulation of Sizes and Weight of Motor Vehicles,* 77th Cong., 1st sess., H. Doc. 354, 1941, p. 59.

Table 2.9 depicts the divergent weight formulas in existence during 1941 and further illustrates the early disparity in this important aspect of the size and weight area.

The U.S. Interstate Commerce Commission, during an ex parte analysis of the necessity for federal regulation of motor-truck sizes and weights in 1941, summarized a quarter century of state development in the field of sizes and weight and concluded:

> That there are wide and inconsistent variations in the limitations imposed by the several states on the sizes and weights of motor vehicles engaged in the transportation of persons and property upon the public highway. The variations are particularly marked in the limitations which relate to length and weights.
>
> That the limitations of a single state may and often do have an influence and effect which extend, so far as interstate commerce is concerned, far beyond the borders of that state, nullifying or impairing the effectiveness of more liberal limitations imposed by neighboring states.

That with respect to the public highways which serve as the principal arteries of interstate commerce, state limitations may be, and to a considerable extent probably are, less liberal than is necessary for the proper protection of the highways and their appurtenances and of public safety.

That where such conditions exist, the limitations operate as an obstacle to the flow of interstate traffic, render motor transportation more costly, and result in an impairment of service to the public.[29]

Even though the commission asserted that a fundamental need for federal regulation of motor-vehicle sizes and weights had been clearly demonstrated, another 15 years would transpire before Congress would concur with this observation.

During the interval that encompassed World War II, many states moderated their respective weight restrictions and frequently permitted overloading of vehicles. Of course, the experience gleaned in wartime operations was a major contributing factor in the acceptance and adoption of revised AASHO policy in April 1926. This policy has been previously depicted in Table 2.8. The revised policy indicated cognizance of serious deficiencies contained in the previous policy and thereby provided several significant modifications from the recommendations that the association had originally embraced in 1932. First, group axle loads were redefined relative to bridge capacity, particularly the H-15 design, which predominated the main road systems of the states; second, utilization of a single value for "C" was deemed impractical; and last, a table of maximum weights permitted in relation to the spacing of any group of axles eliminated employing a mathematical equation as a device for weight regulation.[30]

Unlike the widespread indifference that the 1932 recommendations confronted, the 1946 policy rapidly resolved in developing a positive propensity in state legislation. Whereas in 1944, 12 years after the genesis of AASHO policy introduction, the status of only 26 states restricted maximum gross vehicle weight by mathematical formula, by 1950, 35 states had enacted legislation that included a formula or a table of weights predicated on the 1946 policy table.[31]

Although between 1923 and 1949 an inordinate amount of research augmented and refined the body of knowledge derived from the Bates road tests, such investigations were primarily undertaken by individual state agencies functioning in an independent capacity.[32] No replications or further tests occurred that acutally involved loading of pavements of known character and dimensions with traffic of precisely known weight. Therefore, when Road Test One-Maryland was advocated and subsequently conducted as a specific test and as a cooperative venture involving several midwestern and eastern states in 1950, highway authorities, trucking companies, and other transportation interests ardently awaited the results.

Road Test One-Maryland was administered in a six-month period extending from June to December 1950 on a 1.1 mile section of U.S. Highway 301 located near LaPlata, Maryland. The research test was supervised by the Highway Research Board. Principle focus of the important experiment was to discern the relative impact of four different axle loads on an existing concrete pavement. The loads employed in Road Test One-Maryland were 18 and 22.4 kips on a single axle and 32 and 44.8 kips on tandem-axle vehicles. Basically, the test results suggested that the heavier axle loads were accompanied by more cracking and joint depression. The real significance of Road Test One-Maryland resided in the fact that much of the eastern and midwestern section of the nation had at least some indication of the effects of various axle loads on concrete pavements under climatic and soil conditions similar to those in the test region.[33] Unfortunately, the Maryland results were deficient in two respects: first, other geographical sections of the country were not provided valid information pertinent to the impact of axle loadings for soil and climatic conditions in their respective area; and second, the entire nation still remained without empirical test data regarding other types of subbase, base, and surfacing designs.[34]

In June 1951, the Western Association of State Highway Officials (WASHO) sponsored a resolution providing for the construction and testing of a road representative of both the climate and soil of the western United States. This particular project, designated the WASHO Road Test, was designed to ascertain the effect of various axle loads on certain designs of flexible pavements. The WASHO Road Test, conducted from November 1953 through May 1954, provided the participating states with invaluable data that could be utilized not only to estimate vehicle loading and size restrictions, but likewise the design of pavement structures.[35]

Including the planning stages, the AASHO Road Test was conducted from 1951–60, and constituted the third full-scale test of pavement behavior under controlled truck traffic administered by the Highway Research Board. This test remains the most comprehensive study regarding the performance of highway pavement structures of known thickness under moving loads of known magnitude and frequency.[36] Although the fact that pavement life was affected by numerous variables, such as axle loads and number of load applications, was generally known, the $27 million[37] AASHO project manifested the extent to which performance modification was affiliated with any specific change in axle load and number of repetitions thereof. Furthermore, the test findings pertinent to the relationship existing between load and performance furnished objective data for establishing an equitable, higher user-tax structure. Besides the emergence of the serviceability concept as a new method of evaluating pavement performance, the equivalence of single- and tandem-axle arrangements was ascertained. Last, of the theoretical predictions concerning deflection and strain on bridges, many were substantiated by the test results.[38]

On July 1, 1956, just before beginning the construction of the special test facilities for the AASHO Road Test, Congress passed the landmark Federal-Aid Highway Act of 1956 and the federal government thereby entered the field of motor-vehicle weights and dimensions. Congress obviously recognized that size and weight maximums were fundamentally an administrative problem of the various state governments but contended that if the federal government was committed to 90 percent of the cost of interstate-system improvements, then it was entitled to protect this investment against possible damage arising from heavy loads using the highway.[39] Subsection 108(j)* of the act established maximum weight and width limitations for vehicles, as well as the following penalty for violations:

> (j) MAXIMUM WEIGHT AND WIDTH LIMITATIONS—No funds authorized to be appropriated for any fiscal year by this section shall be apportioned to any State within the boundaries of which the Interstate System may lawfully be used by vehicles with weight in excess of eighteen thousand pounds carried on any one axle, or with a tandem axle weight in excess of thirty-two thousand pounds, or with an overall gross weight in excess of 73,280 pounds, or with a width in excess of 96 inches, or the corresponding maximum weights or maximum widths permitted for vehicles using the public highways of such State under laws or regulations established by appropriate State authority in effect on July 1, 1956, whichever is the greater. Any amount which is withheld from apportionment to any State pursuant to the foregoing provisions shall lapse: Provided, however, that nothing herein shall be construed to deny apportionment to any State allowing the operation within such State of any vehicles or combinations thereof that could be lawfully operated within such state on July 1, 1956.[40]

The prescribed limitations of subsection 108(j) were simply the 1946 AASHO policy on weights and dimensions, as illustrated in Table 2.8. This subsection obviously was not an attempt by Congress to preempt the prerogative of state legislatures, but instead to implement a supervision on further size and weight increases, pending the results of several research tests currently in progress.[41] Subsection 108(k) states:

> (k) TESTS TO DETERMINE MAXIMUM DESIRABLE DIMENSIONS AND WEIGHTS—The Secretary of Commerce is directed to take all action possible to expedite the conduct of a series of tests now planned or being

---

*Now Title 23, Section 127, *United States Code.*

conducted by the Highway Research Board of the National Academy of Sciences, in cooperation with the Bureau of Public Roads, the several States, and other persons and organizations, for purposes of determining the maximum desirable dimensions and weights for vehicles operated on the Federal-aid highway systems, including the Interstate System, and, after the conclusion of such tests, but not later than March 1, 1959, to make recommendations to the Congress with respect to such maximum desirable dimensions and weights.[42]

Congress obviously desired the empirical results of the AASHO Road Test prior to reaching a final decision regarding size and weight maximums for the interstate system.

The grandfather provision contained in subsection 108(j) of the federal act that permitted exceptions to the prescribed width and three weight maximums in those states where greater limits were lawfully permitted on July 1, 1956, was significant to the future consideration of motor-vehicle weight and length dimensions. Inasmuch as a number of states had modified their respective standards prior to this federal statute to consolidate gains derived from advancements in highway and vehicle systems, substantial legal exceptions to the specific requirements cited in the 1956 act were present in the federal law.[43] Thus, the Federal-Aid Highway Act of 1956 not only did not assist in alleviating the heterogeneity that pervaded state codes but, rather, perpetuated it.

Primarily due to delays incurred in completing the AASHO Road Test, the final report pursuant to subsection 108(k) was not presented to Congress until August 18, 1964. This report, House Document 354, with the exception of the gross-weight maximum, stated that Section 127, Title 23 of the *United States Code* be retained through June 30, 1967. In referring to the existing maximum gross weight of 73,280 pounds, the report recommended that amendment to Section 127 which would, beginning six months following the enactment of such an amendment to and through June 30, 1967 provide a new table of gross weights[44] based on the general formula $W = 500 (LN/N-1 + 12N + 32)$.* This recommendation was made law on June 30, 1967, without action on the proposed amendment. Interestingly, this particular gross-weight formula had been previously proposed by AASHO in 1951 due to a basic recognition that no single value of "C" in the 1946 formula, nor any single constant in the derived equation on which the 1946 weight table was based, would satisfy the requirements for the range of vehicles and combinations

---

*"W" represented maximum weight in pounds carried in any group of two or more axles; "L" was the distance in feet between the extremes of any group of two or more consecutive axles; and "N" was the number of axles in the group under consideration.

encountered on the highways employing two to six or more axles.[45] But, similar to the federal experience, AASHO was awaiting the final results of various road tests which were either already proposed or in progress. Practically concurrent to the efforts which went into preparation of the federal recommendations, the AASHO Committee on Highway Transport not surprisingly officially adopted its 1951 formula.[46]

Since the Federal-Aid Highway Act of 1956, several sessions of Congress have contemplated various proposed revisions to the size and weight limits of motor vehicles utilizing the interstate system. During the second session of the 90th Congress, Senate Bill S. 2658 made provisions to increase the single-axle limit from 18,000 to 20,000 pounds, the tandem-axle limit from 32,000 to 34,000 pounds, the width restriction from 96 to 102 inches, and the gross-weight maximums to be determined by the formula $W = 500 \, (LN/N-1 + 12N + 36)$.[47] Although this bill passed the Senate, it was subsequently defeated in the House of Representatives. During the first session of the 91st Congress, two proposals, H.R. 11870 and H.R. 11619, were considered, and both legislative proposals would have amended Section 127 of Title 23 of the *United States Code*. Even though H.R. 11870 was similar in composition to S. 2658, the House bill provided for an increase in the permissible width of motor buses.[48] Even though extensive hearings were conducted in 1969 before the Subcommittee on Roads, both bills failed to pass the 91st Congress. The motor-carrier industry and other proponents of size and weight change were preoccupied with the economic aspect of the bills and failed to adequately address the safety aspect.

In the years following federal entry into the size and weight field and subsequent years of legislative debates, several significant research projects were completed and published. Two of these projects are germane to this analysis. In 1961, a 1955–56 study conducted by Hoy Stevens was published that investigated the changes in vehicle-mile costs and in payload ton-mile costs as gross weights of trailer combinations were increased.[49] This particular study was upgraded thereafter to reflect economic conditions of 1964.[50] Although the data produced from these two investigations represented an important contribution in the area of comparative operating costs of highway freight vehicles, it failed to confront the question of simply what the economic end point in gross weights is. These and other questions relative to establishing optimum limits of weights and dimensions were explored by Winfrey and others during the interval 1964–68 and published in 1974. The Winfry Study discovered the following sizes and weights to be optimal:

1. A vehicle height of 13.5 feet.
2. A vehicle width of 102 inches.
3. Axle weight limits of 22/38 kips, single/tandem axles for universal use.
4. A gross weight limit of at least 120,000 pounds.[51]

The shift in equilibrium of the U.S. economic philosophy from abundance to scarcity in 1973[52] transformed the legislative momentum from failure to success for the motor-carrier industry. Given the fuel shortage and decreased truck productivity, in early 1974 the Federal Highway Administration seriously began considering the economical engineering feasibility of proposing legislation that would liberalize truck size and weight restrictions on the interstate system.[53]

Trucks, like automobiles, were legally compelled not to exceed 55 mph. This speed requirement, when combined with the 10-hour maximum driving limit imposed by the Bureau of Motor Carrier Safety,[54] diminished the distance that goods could be hauled each day.[55] While the possibility of extending hours of service was considered in order to compensate for the loss of productivity caused by the lower speed limit, the concept was quickly discarded as an alternative on safety grounds.*

In response to the growing public concern regarding energy and transportation difficulties, the Transportation Subcommittee of the Senate Public Works Committee began hearings on February 20, 1974, that explored the plausibility of possibly increasing motor-vehicle size and weight limitations.[56] In August, the industry received a temporary setback when Representative Edward I. Koch's (D-N.Y.) amendment struck the weight language from H.R. 12859, the Federal Mass Transportation Act of 1974, before the bill was sent to the Senate.[57] However, on December 18, the House and Senate passed and forwarded to the White House S. 3934, a bill that essentially provided for a larger authorization of funds for rural roads and highways, extended the 55-mph speed limit, and permitted heavier trucks to operate on the interstate system. The legislation contained provisions that increased the single-axle, truck-weight limit from 18,000 to 20,000 pounds, the tandem-axle weight limit from 32,000 to 34,000 pounds, and the gross vehicle weight limit from 73,280 to 80,000 pounds. States that then maintained higher weight limits on noninterstate highways, moreover, would be permitted to adopt those weight standards for their segments of the interstate system.[58] This bill became P.L. 93-643 on January 4, 1975.

PRODUCTIVITY

The U.S. Department of Labor broadly defines productivity as a concept that expresses the association between the quantity of goods manufactured (output) and the quantity of labor, capital, land, energy, and other resources

---

*From a statement by Kenneth L. Pierson, Deputy Director, Bureau of Motor Carrier Safety, in a personal interview on July 31, 1975.

that produced it (input).[59] In a general sense, productivity is measured in one of two ways. One method ties output to a composite of inputs, weighted in such a fashion that their relative importance is reflected.[60] For a motor carrier, productivity of the intercity line-haul operation is governed to a large extent by various state and federal statutes pertaining to vehicle size, weight, and speed. That is, intercity motor carrier productivity is a dual function of pay-load and transit time. The major problems relevant to productivity of the intercity operation will now be considered.

The first comprehensive investigation of tonnage and shipping densities of freight transported by highway was conducted during the mid-1950s by Malcolm F. Kent. He ascertained the primary pattern of the pertinent shipping-density characteristics of several commodities moved by highway carrier and the relationship of payloads of various commodities to the gross weights of practical highway freight vehicles.[61] Since Kent's initial study, motor carriers have demonstrated substantial increases in tons of output per unit of input and productivity has normally been expressed as dollars of output per dollar of labor costs. Or, alternatively stated, productivity has been shown as output per man hour, man day, or man month of labor. The productivity measure has often been an index number, depicting a trend over a period of time, registering only relative change without accounting for causes of change. Therefore, several factors, such as improved organization, technological innovations, more highly skilled labor, increased vehicle size or weight, the use of more efficient equipment, and the substitution of labor for other factors of production, have been identified as influencing productivity. Nevertheless, in the motor carrier industry no studies have been conducted that completely isolate the contributing factors in increasing productivity.[62] This observation raises two inquiries: first, what specific factors have affected intercity trucking productivity; and second, how can this productivity be appropriately and accurately measured.

One significant, critical development in intercity productivity has been the growth in capacity resulting from the use of larger trucks. Not only has the average length of a new trailer increased from 32.5 feet in 1953 as compared to 40 feet in 1974, but twin trailers, which offer the added capacity of two short trailers (24 to 28 feet), are presently permitted to engage in commercial operations in 35 states.[63] Twin-trailer equipment provides for up to 33 percent more transport productivity per vehicle combination without a simultaneous increase in vehicle weight. Increased cubic capacity consitutes a quintessential factor simply because presently freight has demonstrated a propensity toward lighter weights and bulkier sizes. As a result of this trend the difficulty of loading tractor semitrailer units to achieve maximum weight utilization and proper axle loading has intensified.[64]

A technological innovation occurring outside of the motor-carrier industry that has certainly contributed to improving both the efficiency and produc-

tivity of trucking operations has been the effective adoption and employment
of computer technology. Elaborate information systems permit management
to trace shipments and obtain empirical data, such as delivery time, type and
weight of freight, location of trucks, and destination of freight. Also, the
electronic computer has automatically facilitated a wide range of revenue and
accounting functions.[65] Other external factors necessarily include the evolution of specialized trucks that are more effective in the loading and unloading
of various commodities* and the expansion of the interstate highway system,
which has particularly facilitated both scheduling and delivery.[66]

Conversely, size and weight regulations imposed by state and federal laws
regarding the use of the system serve as examples of direct impediments to
improved carrier productivity.[67] Not only are the regulations fundamentally
a hinderance, but there is considerable deviation from the federal statutory
limits due to the grandfather clause contained in the 1956 act. For example,
before passage of the 1974 legislation, over 50 percent of the states maintained
statutory and/or legal limits beyond the single-axle limitations, whereas 60
percent exceeded the tandem-axle restrictions.

The 1974 law, moreover, does not specifically compel any state to modify
its size and weight laws but instead merely provides parameters that a state
cannot surpass. Only a few states have since adopted the present new limitations and the ultimate intentions of other states have yet to be demonstrated.
Even if all states for which the law proved to be expedient took advantage of
the 1974 augmentations, there would still remain 14 states with higher single-
axle restrictions and 17 states with higher tandem-axle restrictions.[68]

The only other federal size and weight regulations apply to gross vehicle
weight and width on vehicles utilizing the interstate system. Although 15 states
maintain gross weight limits in excess of 73,280 pounds, only a few states
permit gross weight to exceed 80,000 pounds. In terms of carrier productivity,
this regulation has generally resulted in a motor-carrier loading for the state
that has had the most stringent weight or dimension restrictions. Width, on
the other hand, curtails productivity for trucks that are volume—not weight
—limited. It is generally estimated that approximately 50 percent of the 75
million pallets produced annually in the United States are of the 40- by 48-inch
variety. As previously indicated, the recommendation for increasing the width
limitation from 96 to 102 inches originated in the 1964 report entitled "Maximum Desirable Dimensions and Weights of Vehicles Operated on the Federal-
Aid Systems" and has continued to appear in almost all subsequent legislative
proposals pertinent to size and weight. Although never enacted by Congress,

---

*Many motor-carrier firms, such as Arkansas Best Freight and Jones Trucking Lines, have
special commodity divisions that utilize specially designed equipment.

those six additional inches of truck cargo width would permit the 40- by-48-inch pallets to be loaded by carriers two units wide. Dependent upon the various length restriction enforced by each state, this action would translate into an increase in pallet capacity of up to 30 percent and in turn would permit the addition of several engineering developments that would enhance safety and fuel economy.[69]

Even though the federal limits are applicable only to the interstate system, up until the early 1970s all states maintained restrictions on their major highways that coincided with the federal maximums, thereby effectively making the federal regulations the state limits. Prior to the 1974 legislation, however, a number of states enacted laws that authorized the carrying of weight above the federal limits on noninterstate highways, thus creating an anomalous situation where the interstate system, which is generally constructed to the highest standards, was restricted to vehicles lighter than those tolerated on other roads.[70]

The measurement of productivity essentially involves two fundamental problems that are germane to both input and output data. First, there is considerable difficulty in obtaining direct quantity measures of output and input, and thus substitute measures or approximations must frequently be utilized. Second, since most data are gathered for purposes other than productivity measurement, established definitions and procedures for reporting information on production and factor inputs must therefore be employed. These may or may not be consistent with concepts appropriate for productivity measurement.[71] The issue of productivity measurement received prominent attention at a conference sponsored by the Interstate Commerce Commission (ICC) on November 26, 1974, in Washington, D.C.[72]

In the motor-carrier industry a significant portion of the impasse that surrounds the measurement of productivity stems from disagreement over the proper components of productivity. This factor was shown at the ICC Conference, as interpretations of transportation productivity varied to embrace inputs such as labor, capital, energy, machinery, materials, profitability, and the value of service rendered to the shipper or shipping public.[73] In this regard, relating output to a single input such as factor cost was totally inadequate in view of the numerous combinations of input factors. The area of output was just as confused with respect to what was being measured, that is, transit time, pickup and delivery service, ton-miles or highway miles, or damage factors.[74]

Unequivocally, the output of a firm engaged in transportation is difficult to measure and characterize. But a standard measure is the quantity of cargo ton-miles produced. Unfortunately, this measure does not take into account the size of shipment, commodity, or empty backhauls. Apparently, any attempt to consolidate several attributes into a single variable will result in the glossing over of some aspects.[75] Even though extensive debate exists considering the appropriateness of the ton-mile in measuring output,[76] there is general agreement that while it is not perfect, is is the most appropriate unit of measurement.[77] Even if output is disaggregated into several components—such as pickup and delivery, platform, billing and collecting, and line-hauling —there is little question that the ton-mile emerges as most relevant to the line-haul or intercity freight movement.[78]

NOTES

1. Armand J. Salmon, Jr. et al. *Financing Highways* (Princeton: Tax Institute, 1957), p. 185. See also Charles A. Taff, *Commercial Motor Transportation,* 3rd ed. (Homewood, Ill.: R. D. Irwin, 1961), chap. 3.

2. Edna Trull, *Borrowing for Highways* (New York: Dun and Bradstreet, 1937), p. 3.

3. U.S., House, *Congressional Record,* 64th Cong., 1st sess., December 6, 1915–January 13, 1916, 53, pt. 1: 98.

4. U.S., Congress, House, Committee on Ways and Means, *Revenue Bill of 1918,* Report No. 767, 65th Cong., 2d sess., September 3, 1918, pp. 33–34.

5. F. G. Crawford, *The Gasoline Tax in the United States* (Chicago: Public Administration Service, 1936), p. 7.

6. Edmund P. Learned, *State Gasoline Taxes,* Bulletin of the University of Kansas Humanistic Studies, vol. 26, no. 6 (Lawrence, Kans.: University of Kansas, 1925), p. 9.

7. Wilfred Owen, *A Study in Highway Economics* (Cambridge, Mass.: Alpha Chapter of Massachusetts, Phi Beta Kappa, 1934), p. 86.

8. Oregon, *General Laws,* chap. 159 (1919), pp. 219–23.

9. U.S., Public Roads Administration, *Highway Practice in the United States of America* (Washington, D.C.: Government Printing Office, 1949), p. 30.

10. U.S., Department of Transportation, Federal Highway Administration, Bureau of Public Roads, *Highway Statistics, Summary to 1965* (Washington, D.C.: Government Printing Office, 1967), p. 17.

11. U.S., Department of Transportation, Federal Highway Administration, "News," FHWA 94–75 (October 6, 1975).

12. F. G. Crawford, *The Administration of the Gasoline Tax in the United States,* 3rd ed. (New York: Municipal Administration Service, 1932), pp. 58–59.

13. Learned, op. cit., p. 27. Several excellent summaries of the significant court rulings of the 1920s exist. See, for example, F. G. Crawford, *The Administration of the Gasoline Tax in the United States,* pp. 58–64. Additionally, the annual reports of the North American Gasoline Tax Conference for the years from 1926 to present provide a yearly synopsis of noteworthy motor-fuels tax legislation.

14. F. G. Crawford, *Motor Fuel Taxation in the United States* (Baltimore: Lord Baltimore Press, 1939), p. 42.

15. Salmon, op. cit., p. 187.

16. Crawford, *Motor Fuel Taxation in the United States,* pp. 68–69.

17. U.S., Public Roads Administration, Federal Works Agency, *Highway Statistics, Summary to 1945* (Washington, D.C.: Government Printing Office, 1947), p. 1. This excludes motor fuel purchased by the federal government.

18. *United States Code,* vol. 6, 1970 ed. (Washington, D.C.: Government Printing Office, 1971), p. 6,009.

19. See Crawford, *Motor Fuel Taxation in the United States,* pp. 71–75.

20. U.S., Department of Transportation, Federal Highway Administration, *Road User and Property Taxes on Selected Motor Vehicles* (Washington, D.C.: Government Printing Office, 1973), p. 1.

21. U.S., Department of Transportation, Federal Highway Administration, Bureau of Public Roads, *The Role of Third Structure Taxes in the Highway User Tax Family* (Washington, D.C.: Government Printing Office, 1968), p. 42.

22. Jess N. Rosenberg, "Motor Carrier Comments," in *North American Gasoline Tax Conference, Twenty-Eighth Annual Report* (Chicago: Evans Printing Company, 1954), p. 60.

23. Randall A. Rinquest, "Current Legal Problems in the Motor Fuel Tax Field," in *North American Gasoline Tax Conference, Forty-Third Annual Report* (Chicago: Evans Printing Company, 1969), p. 52.

24. Jess N. Rosenberg, "Trucking Views on Highway Tax Equities," in *North American Gasoline Tax Conference, Thirty-Seventh Annual Report* (Chicago: Evans Printing Company, 1963), pp. 15–16; U.S., Department of Transportation, *The Role of Third Structure Taxes in the Highway User Tax Family,* p. 41.

25. B. M. Hutchinson, B. A. Sanders, and W. D. Glauz, *Effects of Current State Licensing, Permit, and Fee Requirements on Motor Trucks Involved in Interstate Commerce* (Washington, D.C.: Federal Highway Administration, Department of Transportation, 1975), p. 9.

26. Hutchinson, Sanders, and Glauz, op. cit., p. 10.

27. The history of the size and weight problem prior to 1940 is adopted, except where noted, from U.S., Department of Transportation, Federal Highway Administration, *Review of Safety and Economic Aspects of Increased Vehicle Sizes and Weights* (Washington, D.C.: Federal Highway Administration, 1969), pp. 10–26. For a detailed history of the Federal Department of Transportation see Grant M. Davis, *The Department of Transportation* (Lexington, Mass.: D. C. Heath, 1974), chaps. 1–6.

28. A. E. Johnson, ed., *AASHO—The First Fifty Years—1914–1964* (Washington, D.C.: American Association of State Highway Officials, 1965), pp. 40–41.

29. U.S., Congress, *Federal Regulation of Sizes and Weight of Motor Vehicle,* p. 25.

30. U.S., Department of Transportation, *Review of Safety and Economic Aspects of Increased Vehicle Sizes and Weights,* pp. 16–17.

31. U.S., Congress, Senate, Committee on Interstate and Foreign Commerce, Subcommittee on Land and Water Transportation, *Study of Domestic Land and Water Transportation,* Hearing, 81st Cong., 2d sess., April 4–July 28, 1950, pp. 988–89.

32. Edward C. Grubbs, *A Review of Literature Pertaining to the Development, Subsequent Evaluations and Current Use of the General AASHO Road Test Equation,* Technical Report No. 1, Highway Research Project No. 20, Arkansas State Highway Department Planning and Research Division (Fayetteville, Ark.: University of Arkansas, 1965), p. 3.

33. Highway Research Board, *Road Test One—MD, Final Report,* Special Report 4 (Washington, D.C.: National Academy of Sciences-National Research Council, 1952), pp. 5–11, 75–77.

34. Grubbs, op. cit., p. 6.

35. Highway Research Board, *The WASHO Road Test, Part 2: Test Data, Analyses, Findings,* Special Report 22 (Washington, D.C.: National Academy of Sciences-National Research Council, 1955), pp. 1–5.

36. Highway Research Board, *The AASHO Road Test, History and Description of Project,* Special Report 61A (Washington, D.C.: National Academy of Sciences-National Research Council, 1961), p. v.

37. Highway Research Board, *The AASHO Road Test, Proceedings of a Conference Held May 16–18, 1962, St. Louis, Mo.,* Special Report 73 (Washington, D.C.: National Academy of Sciences-National Research Council, 1962), pp. 9–10.

38. Highway Research Board, *The AASHO Road Test, Report 7, Summary Report,* Special Report 61G (Washington, D.C.: National Academy of Sciences-National Research Council, 1962), pp. 1–4.

39. U.S., Congress, House, Committee on Public Works, *Federal-Aid Highway and Highway Revenue Acts of 1956,* 84th Cong., 2d sess., H. Rept. 2022, 1956, p. 10.

40. Ibid., H. Rept. 2436, pp. 8–9.

41. U.S., Department of Transportation, *Review of Safety and Economic Aspects of Increased Vehicle Sizes and Weights,* p. 22.

42. U.S., Congress, *Federal-Aid Highway and Highway Revenue Acts of 1956,* p. 9.

43. U.S., Congress, House, *Maximum Desirable Dimensions and Weights of Vehicles Operated on the Federal-Aid Systems,* 88th Cong., 2d sess., H. Doc. 354, 1964, p. 11.

44. Ibid., p. 3.

45. U.S., Department of Transportation, *Review of Safety and Economic Aspects of Increased Vehicle Sizes and Weights,* p. 19.

46. American Association of State Highway Officials, Committee on Highway Transport, *Policy on Maximum Dimensions and Weights of Motor Vehicles to be Operated Over the Highways of the United States* (n.p., 1963), p. 17.

47. U.S., Congress, Senate, Committee on Public Works, Subcommittee on Roads, *Vehicle Sizes and Weights,* Hearing, 90th Cong., 2d sess., February 19–21 and March 7, 1968, p. 5.

48. U.S., Congress, House, Committee on Public Works, Subcommittee on Roads, *Vehicle Weight and Dimension Limitations,* Hearing, 91st Cong., 1st sess., July 8–September 4, 1969, pp. 2–6. For an in-depth analysis of transportation safety, consult Grant M. Davis and Martin T. Farris, "Federal Transportation Safety Programs—Misdirected Emphasis and Wasted Resources," *Transportation Journal* 11, no. 4 (Summer 1972): 5–17; Grant M. Davis, "One Way to Improve Trucking Safety," *The Arizona Roadrunner* 22, no. 4 (April 1969): 6–8; and Grant M. Davis, "Proposed Federal Changes in Interstate Highway Route Selection and Design," *Alabama Business* 39, no. 9 (May 15, 1969): 1–3.

49. See Hoy Stevens, *Line-Haul Trucking Costs in Relation to Vehicle Gross Weights,* Highway Research Board, Bulletin 301 (Washington, D.C.: National Academy of Sciences, National Research Council, 1961).

50. See Hoy Stevens, "Line-Haul Trucking Costs Upgraded, 1964," Highway Research Record, no. 127 (Washington, D.C.: Highway Research Board, 1966).

51. Robley Winfrey et al., *Economics of the Maximum Limits of Motor Vehicle Dimensions and Weights*, 2 vols. (Washington, D.C.: Federal Highway Administration, Department of Transportation, 1974), 1:53.

52. I. W. Abel, " 'Suddenly' There's an Energy Crisis," *Viewpoint* 3 (Fourth Quarter, 1973): 1.

53. "FHWA Studies Truck Size-Weight Move to Conserve Fuel, Increase Productivity," *Traffic World* 157 (February 4, 1974): 85.

54. *Federal Motor Carrier Safety Regulations,* Title 49, Section 395.3 (Washington, D.C.: Government Printing Office, October 1, 1974), p. 85. U.S., Department of Transportation, Federal Highway Administration, Bureau of Motor Carrier Safety.

55. Albert R. Karr, "Whoosh! Here Come the Big Rigs," *Wall Street Journal,* December 17, 1974, p. 14, col. 4. For an in-depth discussion of the impact of reduced speed limits and efficient operations, consult Grant M. Davis, Martin T. Farris, and Jack J. Holder, Jr., *Management of Transportation Carriers* (New York: Praeger, 1975), chap. 8.

56. See U.S., Congress, Senate, Committee on Public Works, Subcommittee on Transportation, *Transportation and the New Energy Policies (Truck Sizes and Weights),* Part 2, Hearing 93rd Cong., 2d sess., February 20–21 and March 26, 1974.

57. "Truck Weight Increase Vetoed," *Traffic Topics,* September–October 1974, p. 14.

58. "House and Senate Approve Federal-Aid Highway Bill, Raise Truck Weight Limits," *Traffic World* 160 (December 23, 1974): 9.

59. U.S., Department of Labor, Bureau of Labor Statistics, *Productivity and the Economy,* Bulletin 1779 (Washington, D.C.: Government Printing Office, 1973), p. 1.

60. U.S., Department of Labor, *Productivity and the Economy,* p. 1.

61. Malcolm F. Kent, "The Freight's the Weight," *Proceedings of the Thirty-Seventh Annual Meeting of the Highway Research Board, January 6–10, 1958* (Washington, D.C.: National Academy of Sciences, National Research Council, 1958), p. 21.

62. U.S., Department of Transportation, *Review of Safety and Economic Aspects of Increased Vehicle Sizes and Weights,* p. 184.

63. Richard B. Carnes, "Productivity Trends in Intercity Trucking," *Monthly Labor Review* 97 (January 1974): 55.

64. American Trucking Associations, "The Case for Twin Trailers," 4th ed. (1974), pp. 1–3.

65. Walter A. Collymore, "Computer Technology: A Key to Improved Productivity in Transportation," *Traffic World* 762 (June 23, 1975): 35–36.

66. Carnes, op. cit., pp. 55–56.

67. Rodger F. Ringham, " 'Reguflation'—The Trauma of Truck Transport," *Traffic World* 162 (June 23, 1975): 51.

68. See "State Legal Maximum Dimensions and Weights of Motor Vehicles Compared with AASHTO Standards," prepared by the American Association of State Highway and Transportation Officials (n.p., December 21, 1974).

69. Ringham, op. cit., pp. 51–52.

70. "What Shippers Should Know About Truck Size and Weight Limits," *Traffic World* 154 (June 25, 1973): 33.

71. U.S., Department of Labor, Bureau of Labor Statistics, *The Meaning and Measurement of Productivity,* Bulletin 1714 (Washington, D.C.,: Government Printing Office, 1971), pp. 9–10.

72. *Proceedings of the Interstate Commerce Commission's Productivity Measurement Conference on November 26, 1974* (Washington, D.C.: Government Printing Office, 1975).

73. *Proceedings,* op. cit., pp. 35–48, 92–96.

74. *Proceedings,* op. cit., p. 94.

75. Leland S. Case and Lester B. Lave. "Inland Waterway Transportation: Some Evidence on Cost," in *Criteria for Transport Pricing,* eds. Marvin L. Fair and James R. Nelson (Cambridge, Md.: Cornell Maritime Press, 1973), p. 66.

76. For dissenting opinions see Theodore Quast, "The Output Unit in Transportation," *Transportation Journal* 10 (Winter 1970): 5–7; and Allan C. Flott, Lana R. Bates, and Ronald D. Roth, "The Ton-Mile, Does it Properly Measure Transportation Output?," Presentation to the Transportation Research Board, Commission on Societal Technologies, National Research Council (Washington, D.C.: Department of Research and Transport Economics, American Trucking Association, 1975), pp. 1-12.

77. George W. Wilson, *Essays on Some Unsettled Questions in the Economics of Transportation* (Bloomington, Ind.: Indiana University, Foundation for Economic and Business Studies, 1962), pp. 14–23.

78. Darwin W. Diacoff, "Analyzing 'Productivity Trends in Intercity Trucking'," *Monthly Labor Review* 97 (October 1974): 41.

3

THE CURRENT STATUS OF
WEIGHT AND DIMENSION REGULATION

This chapter analyzes in depth the existing state and federal statutory provisions governing sizes and weights under which motor vehicles must operate in the United States, elucidating the issue of uniformity. However, before this can be properly ascertained, the significance of weight and dimension standards to motor carriers should be placed in a proper perspective. In this regard, two questions that have been posed and investigated previously in another investigation shall be reviewed and reconsidered. These queries focus essentially upon how many motor vehicles are affected by maximum vehicle standards and what portion of the domestic freight they transport.[1]

Employing 1960–66 data, John Fuller proffered the following observations regarding weight and size restrictions: larger and heavier motor vehicles constituted no more than 1 percent of the total number of motor vehicles; these vehicles transported slightly over 3 percent of the intercity ton-miles and were involved in perhaps 4 percent of all motor-vehicle miles of travel; and the share of the total freight-operating revenue gained through transport by larger and heavier trucks constituted less than 6 percent of the intercity total.[2] Several of these calculations are in need of careful scrutiny.

Fuller's approximation of the number of vehicles affected by maximum size and weight regulation was predicated entirely upon state motor-vehicle registrations for 1965 and included diesel commercial buses and tractor-trucks, as shown in Table 3.1. The principle deficiency in Fuller's particular approach was that he apparently only considered one maximum weight, that is, gross vehicle weight, when in reality three exist. Single- and tandem-axle weights are actually restrictive since no two-, three-, or four-axle vehicle can legally or logically achieve the gross weight maximum because of pertinent

TABLE 3.1

State Motor Vehicle Registrations, 1965

Motor Vehicle Type	Number Registered	Percent of Registrations
Automobiles	75,260,847	82.026
Buses	314,284	.342
(Diesel commercial buses)	(61,159)	(.066)
Motorcycles	1,381,956	1.506
Trucks	14,795,051	16.125
(tractor-trucks)	(736,302)	(.802)
Total	91,752,138	100

Note: Parentheses indicate vehicles potentially restricted by maximum vehicle standards.
Source: U.S., Congress, *Congressional Record,* 90th Cong., 2d sess., July 24, 1968, 114, pt. 18: 23,178, citing U.S., Department of Transportation, Federal Highway Administration, Bureau of Public Roads, *Highway Statistics, 1965* (Washington, D.C.: Government Printing Office, 1967), pp. 33, 35c.

single- and tandem-axle limitations. Therefore, many of these vehicles are actually considered by weights considerably beneath permissible gross vehicle weight and could therefore benefit from either a single- or tandem-axle increase. Although Fuller basically acknowledges that certain single-unit vehicles could conceivably be influenced by maximum weight and dimension restrictions, his mathematical calculations eliminated these vehicles from consideration for all practical purposes.* In this regard, Table 3.2 depicts the absolute magnitude of error derived from this minimization. In 1962, fully one-third of single-unit trucks could be realistically affected by increases in motor-vehicle sizes and weights. This represents nearly 4 million vehicles, as Table 3.2 indicates. Assuming that the proportion of single-unit vehicles influenced by weight and dimension restrictions of 1962 represents a rather crude indicator of the 1972 percentage, the data in Table 3.3 provides additional perception into the crucial question regarding the absolute number of motor vehicles actually restrained by size and weight maximums. Indeed, over 7 million vehicles or 6.023 percent of the total number of vehicles operating domestically may in fact be affected by higher legal weights and dimensions. Although these figures may appear to be relatively insignificant, it is perhaps

---

*Fuller assessed the role of other vehicles as minimal, allowing only .13 percent of all registrations (119,277 vehicles) to account for gasoline-powered buses, other diesel buses, and single-unit vehicles possibly affected by maximum size and weight limitations.

TABLE 3.2

State Motor Vehicle Registrations in 1962,
by Visual Class

Visual Class of Vehicle	Number of Vehicles	Percentage within Class
Automobiles	65,929,000	100
Buses		
Intercity	19,400	6.80
Transit	53,600	18.81
School and other nonrevenue	212,000	74.39
Total	285,000	100
Single-unit trucks		
Two-axle, four-tire	7,941,600	66.67
Two-axle, six-tire*	3,740,200	31.40
Three-axle*	230,600	1.93
Total	11,912,400	100
Trailer combinations, all types*	896,600	100
Total	12,809,000	100

*A total of 4,867,400 trucks (3,970,800 single-unit trucks and 896,000 combinations) may be affected by increases in size and weight regulation.

Sources: U.S., Congress, House, *Maximum Desirable Dimensions and Weights of Vehicles Operated on the Federal-Aid Systems,* 88th Cong., 2d sess., H. Doc. 354, 1964, p. 49.

more appropriate to consider these numbers in terms of homogenous categories, that is, buses within bus categories and trucks within truck categories. Considered in this regard, size and weight restrictions may in reality hinder nearly 22 percent of buses and 36.4 percent of trucks.

The significant question of what material portion of the nation's freight is transported by these vehicles is slightly more complex. Excluding buses entirely, Table 3.4 illustrates that nearly all of the ton-miles hauled by truck on main rural roads in 1961 were conveyed by vehicles possibly affected by size and weight regulation. Again, for lack of more recent empirical evidence, these percentages will be employed in order to approximate the 1972 level of activity. But this methodology creates two relevant questions. First, what segment of aggregate intercity freight is transported by trucks? Second, to what extent is this particular tonnage moved over main rural roads? Table 3.5 furnishes the solution to the initial inquiry and clearly demonstrates that trucks have maintained an average of approximately 22 percent of aggregate intercity freight ton-miles. Preliminary figures indicate a continuation of this trend in 1973.[3] Table 3.6 supplies data pertinent to the second of the questions stipulated above and represents in ton-miles the amount of freight hauled by single-unit trucks and truck combinations on main rural roads.

TABLE 3.3

State Motor Vehicle Registrations, 1972

Vehicle Type	Number of Registrations	Percent within Category	Percent of Total Vehicles
Automobiles	96,859,700	100	80.176
Buses			
Commercial	88,722	21.801	(.073)
School and other	318,232	78.199	—[a]
Total	406,954	100	.337
Single-unit trucks:			
Two-axle, four-tire[b]	12,557,330	66.667	—[a]
Two-axle, six-tire[b]	5,730,670	30.424	(4.744)
Three-axle	548,000	2.909	(.454)
Total	18,836,000	100	—[a]
Truck combinations, all types	909,000	100	(.752)
Total	19,745,000	100	16.344
Motorcycles	3,797,838	100	3.143
Total, all vehicles	120,809,492	—[a]	100

Note: Parentheses indicate categories potentially restricted by maximum vehicle standards.
[a] Dashes indicate not applicable.
[b] Estimated from 1972 two-axle total, using 1962 percentages. (See Table 3.2.)

Sources: Automobile, bus, and motorcycle figures are adopted from U.S., Department of Transportation, Federal Highway Administration, *Highway Statistics, 1972* (Washington, D.C.: Government Printing Office, 1974), p. 33. Truck figures from U.S., Bureau of the Census, Census of Transportation, 1972, *Truck Inventory and Use Survey: U.S. Summary, TC72-T52* (Washington, D.C.: Government Printing Office, 1973), p. 3.

The apparent discrepancy between ton-miles in Table 3.5 and Table 3.6 can be readily explained by the existence of computational differences. Intercity freight, for example, encompasses movement between cities and between rural and urban areas, and excludes rural-to-rural movements and city deliveries.[4] Freight transported on main rural roads during 1972, for instance, consisted of all freight transported over 600,000 miles of designated primary roads in the state highway systems.[5] This mileage, of course, will fluctuate from one year to another. The exact extent to which these totals overlap as well as the precise figures incorporated in one total but not the other simply cannot be accurately established. However, the crucial point is that they are at least roughly compatible.

There are two identifiable trends that are manifest, upon examining data contained in Tables 3.5 and 3.6. Table 3.5 discloses that since 1960 the truck share of intercity freight has remained nearly constant at approximately 22 percent, irrespective of the steady expansion in aggregate ton-miles trans-

TABLE 3.4

Percent of Ton-Miles Hauled on Main Rural Roads in 1961, by Type of Truck

Number of Axles	Truck type	Percentage of Ton-Miles
2	Four-tire, single-unit	4.25
2	Six-tire, single-unit	16.00
3	3A	5.50
3	2S-1	6.75
4	2S-2	39.50
5	3S-2	21.00
4	2-2	1.00
5	3-2	2.00
6 or more	3-3	4.00
Total		100

Sources: Vehicle examples adopted from Robley Winfrey et al., *Economics of the Maximum Limits of Motor Vehicle Dimensions and Weights,* 2 vols. (Washington, D.C.: Federal Highway Administration, Department of Transportation, 1974), 2:10–6. Percentages estimated from Figure 7, U.S., Congress, House, *Maximum Desirable Dimensions and Weights of Vehicles Operated on the Federal-Aid Systems,* 88th Cong., 2d sess., H. Doc. 354, 1964, p. 47.

ported. Thus, the motor-carrier industry's aggregate production output is expanding proportionately to total growth. Table 3.6 indicates that the actual amount of ton-miles hauled by single-unit trucks has persisted at a relatively stable 60 billion ton-miles per annum. Obviously, the expansion in total ton-miles is the direct result of freight increments being moved by truck combinations—larger and heavier trucks.

Table 3.7 represents a consolidation and linear extrapolation of the data previously presented in Tables 3.4 and 3.6, with modifications according to single-axle and combination subtotals occurring in 1972. As motor carriers affected by increases in sizes and weights have been previously designated as all but the two-axle, four-tire category, the apparent vast majority of total ton-miles appears to be hauled by vehicles influenced by size and weight maximums. In fact, Table 3.7 reflects that all except 9.9 billion ton-miles of freight (2.15 percent) are attributable to vehicles potentially affected by weight and dimension regulation, and this in turn translates to 21.7 percent of total intercity freight.[6] The Table 3.8 summary indicates that the number and percent of vehicles potentially influenced by size and weight maximums are significant when analyzed from either a total-vehicle approach or by an alternative individual category.

TABLE 3.5

Intercity Freight by Modes, Selected Years 1960–72
(billions of ton-miles)

Year	Rail		Truck		Oil Pipeline		All Other Modes		Total
	Amount	Percent	Amount	Percent	Amount	Percent	Amount	Percent	
1960	579	44.1	285	2.18	229	17.4	221	16.7	1,314
1965	709	43.3	359	21.9	306	18.7	264	16.7	1,638
1970	771	39.7	412	21.3	431	22.3	322	16.7	1,936
1971	746	38.2	445	22.8	444	22.7	319	16.3	1,954
1972	784	37.7	470	22.7	476	23.0	343	16.6	1,073

Source: Transportation Association of America, *Transportation Facts and Trends* (Washington, D.C.: Transportation Association of America, December 1974), p. 8.

TABLE 3.6

Freight Transported on Main Rural Roads, by Trucks, 1970-72

Year	Single-Unit Truck Billions of Ton-Miles	Percent	Truck Combinations Billions of Ton-Miles	Percent	Total
1960	62	28.3	157	71.7	219
1965	80	29.0	196	71.0	276
1970	41	10.0	371	90.0	412
1971	57	12.3	408	87.7	465
1972	60	13.0	400	87.0	460

Sources: Data for 1960 and 1965 from U.S., Department of Transportation, Federal Highway Administration, Bureau of Public Roads, *Highway Statistics, Summary to 1965* (Washington, D.C.: Government Printing Office, 1967), p. 49; 1970 and 1971 data from U.S., Department of Transportation, Federal Highway Administration, *Highway Statistics, 1972* (Washington, D.C.: Government Printing Office, 1974), p. 55; 1972 data from U.S., Department of Transportation, Federal Highway Administration, *Highway Statistics, 1973* (Washington, D.C.: Government Printing Office, 1975), p. 78.

TABLE 3.7

Freight Transported on Main Rural Roads, by Type of Truck, 1961 and 1972
(billions of ton-miles)

Number of Axles	Truck Category	Percentage of Total Ton-Miles, 1961	Percentage of Truck Category*	Total Ton-Miles 1972
2 (four-tire)	single-axle	4.25	16.50	9.9
2 (six-tire)	single-axle	16.00	62.14	37.3
3	single-axle	5.50	21.36	12.8
		25.75	100	60
3	combination	6.75	9.09	36.4
4	combination	39.50	53.20	212.8
5	combination	21.00	28.28	113.1
4	combination	1.00	1.35	5.4
5	combination	2.00	2.69	10.8
6 or more	combination	4.00	5.39	21.5
		74.25	100	400
		100		460

*Obtained by dividing the column three entry by the appropriate column four subtotal, for example, 25.75 divided by 4.25 gives the percentage of single-axle ton-miles transported by two-axle, four-tire trucks, and so forth.

Source: Compiled by the authors.

TABLE 3.8

Summary of Vehicles Influenced by Size and Weight Maximums

Category	Number of Vehicles Affected	Percent of Total Category	Percent of Total Vehicles
Trucks	7,187,670	36.4	5.95
Buses	88,722	21.8	.07
Total	7,276,392	—	6.02

Source: Compiled by the authors.

MOTOR VEHICLE DIMENSIONS

The dimensions of motor vehicles, which may be considered separately from axle weight, govern the volume of freight that may be physically transported by a specific motor vehicle. From a carrier's perspective, truck width, height, and length influence freight-loading practices, terminal facilities, and the intercity operation. From a pavement-wear standpoint, these four important factors affect pavement and shoulder width, overhead clearance of structures, safety and traffic, and the movement of passenger cars.[7] An important aspect relative to motor-vehicle size and weight dimensions is the utilization of greater cubic capacity. Unfortunately, there is no current data to provide an answer to this crucial question. Nevertheless, several studies, although dated, provide a useful perspective to the above query.

Cubic capacity is predicted upon the duality of vehicle size and the density of the commodity being carried. In this regard, Table 3.9 illustrates some rather typical truck-combination lengths together with their respective cubic capacity. Trucks whose cargo exceeds the physical volume of the carrier before surpassing any of the three weight maximums are generally referred to in trucking industry terminology as "cubing out."

As previously mentioned in Chapter 2, the initial investigation of vehicle space utilization was conducted by Malcolm F. Kent in 1954. He discovered that a 35-foot, van-type cargo body could be loaded visibly full of a commodity weighing up to approximately 24 pounds per cubic foot without exceeding the maximum weight limit.[8] Table 3.10 shows the distribution of tonnage by

TABLE 3.9

Stowage Capacity Related to Lengths of Van-Trailer Combinations

Combination Type	Length in Feet		Total Cargo Stowage Capacity in Cubic Feet
	Overall	Total Cargo Body	
Tractor and semitrailer	45	35	1,880
	50	40	2,150
Truck and full trailer	60	50	2,660
Tractor semitrailer and full trailer	60	50	2,660
	65	54	2,870
	100	80	4,300

Source: Hoy Stevens, *Line-Haul Trucking Costs in Relation to Vehicle Gross Weights,* Highway Research Board, Bulletin 301 (Washington, D.C.: National Academy of Sciences, National Research Council, 1961), p. 14.

TABLE 3.10

Distribution of Tonnage Transported by Highway, by Weight Groups

Commodity Density* in Pounds per Cubic Foot	Percent of Total Tonnage	Cumulative Percent
5.0 - 9.9	1.77	1.77
10.0 - 14.9	3.65	5.42
15.0 - 19.9	.93	6.35
20.0 - 24.9	2.96	9.31
25.0 - 29.9	5.70	15.01
30.0 - 34.9	4.25	19.26
35.0 - 39.9	5.13	24.39
40.0 - 44.9	9.58	33.97
45.0 - 49.9	14.46	48.43
50.0 - 54.9	6.92	55.35
55.0 - 59.9	5.57	60.92
60.0 - 94.9	4.80	65.72
100.0 - 104.9	28.43	94.15
105.0 - 254.9	5.85	100

*No commodities were found in the 95.0 - 99.9 class interval. Average density of all commodities was 66 pounds per cubic foot.

Source: U.S., Congress, House, *Maximum Desirable Dimensions and Weights of Vehicles Operated on the Federal-Aid Systems,* 88th Cong., 2d sess., H. Doc. 354, 1964, p. 64.

weight group, employing Kent's tonnage data. Products possessing a physical density under 25 pounds per cubic foot obviously only comprised 9.31 percent by weight of the total highway haulage, thereby implying that less than 10 percent of the aggregate highway tonnage could benefit from greater dimensions.

A subsequent study differed significantly from Kent's results; in this study 50 percent of all motor-carrier shipments are estimated to be closed out because of the volume factor. In a study of 108 terminals located in 33 states, this same investigation concluded that carrier operating expenses could conceivably be reduced approximately $1 million by never shifting from tractor semitrailer units to twin trailers,[9] that is, permitting additional vehicular cubic capacity. Given that today's general freight shipment by truck averages 12.5 pounds per cubic foot,[10] recent evidence cogently supports the latter study regarding cubic capacity. Tables 3.11 and 3.12 compare cubic capacity data and optimum densities of two typical vehicle combinations that haul general freight. Apparently only the 2-S1-2 configuration with a 102-inch trailer width can attain gross vehicle weight before cubing out if the average general commodity is in fact being transported. This observation also supports an earlier

TABLE 3.11

Cubic Capacity and Optimum Density of the 3-S2 Axle Code Classification under Varying Gross Vehicle Weight Limitations and Two Width Limitations

3-S2 Combination	Based on 96-Inch Trailer Width			Based on 102-Inch Trailer Width		
	g.v.w.[a] 73,280	g.v.w. 78,000	g.v.w. 80,000	g.v.w. 73,280	g.v.w. 78,000	g.v.w. 80,000
40-foot semitrailer						
Tare weight	26,270	26,270	26,270	27,150	27,150	27,150
Tractor	15,270	15,270	15,270	15,770	15,770	15,770
Trailer	11,000	11,000	11,000	11,000	11,000	11,000
Load capacity	47,010	51,730	53,730	46,110	50,830	52,830
Cubic capacity[b]	2,600	2,600	2,600	2,769	2,769	2,769
Optimum density[c]	18.1	19.9	20.7	16.7	18.4	19.1
45-foot semitrailer						
Tare weight	27,020	27,020	27,020	27,970	27,970	27,970
Tractor	15,270	15,270	15,270	15,770	15,770	15,770
Trailer	11,750	11,750	11,750	12,200	12,200	12,200
Load capacity	46,260	50,980	52,980	45,310	50,030	52,030
Cubic capacity[b]	2,925	2,925	2,925	3,115	3,115	3,115
Optimum density[c]	15.8	17.4	18.1	14.5	16.1	16.7

[a] g.v.w. = gross vehicle weight.
[b] In cubic feet.
[c] In pounds per cubic foot, at which each of the trucks would cube out and weigh out simultaneously.

Source: U.S., Department of Transportation, Federal Highway Administration, "Effects of Increasing Truck Size and Weight on Increase in Freight Handling Capacity Per Truck Unit," mimeographed draft (1975), p. 9.

TABLE 3.12

Cubic Capacity and Optimum Density of the 2-S1-2 Axle Code Classification under Varying Gross Vehicle Weight Limitations and Two Width Limitations

2-S1-2 Combination	Based on 96-Inch Trailer Width			Based on 102-Inch Trailer Width		
	g.v.w.[a] 73,280	g.v.w. 80,000	g.v.w. 90,000	g.v.w. 73,280	g.v.w. 80,000	g.v.w. 90,000
Tractor and 27-foot twin trailers						
Tare weight	28,690	28,690	28,690	29,630	29,630	29,630
Tractor	12,223	12,223	12,223	12,573	12,573	12,573
Trailers (two)	7,000[b]	7,000[b]	7,000[b]	7,270[b]	7,270[b]	7,270[b]
Converted dolly	2,467	2,467	2,467	2,517	2,517	2,517
Load capacity	44,950	51,310	61,310	43,650	50,370	60,370
Cubic capacity[c]	3,500	3,500	3,500	3,727	3,727	3,727
Optimum density[d]	12.7	14.7	17.5	11.7	13.5	16.2

[a] g.v.w. = gross vehicle weight.
[b] Weight for each trailer.
[c] In cubic feet.
[d] In pounds per cubic foot, at which each of the trucks would cube out and weigh out simultaneously.

Source: U.S., Department of Transportation, Federal Highway Administration, "Effects of Increasing Truck Size and Weight on Increase in Freight Handling Capacity per Truck Unit," mimeographed draft (1975), p. 9.

statement contained in Chapter 2 with respect to trends toward lighter and bulkier freight. Expanded use of plastics and aluminum in manufacturing processes as well as the adoption of new packaging techniques[11] are responsible for the lower density trends in motor transportation.

There is no precise empirical answer available for the significant question of to what extent greater cubic capacity in vehicles could be utilized. But since the initial studies conducted in 1954 by M. F. Kent, an ever-increasing number of motor trucks have been hindered by cubic capacity. The next section explores the dimensional factors of width, height, and length in order to ascertain their relative economic importance to the trucking industry.

Width

Vehicle width is the only dimensional factor subject to indirect federal jurisdiction and control. As previously discussed in Chapter 2, this indirect control takes the form of apportionment or withholding of federal funds for the construction of federal-aid primary, secondary, urban, and interstate highways. But, it pertains solely to the 42,748 miles[12] of interstate system in the United States as set forth in the Federal-Aid Highway Act of 1956 (P.L. 84-627, Section 108(j), July 1, 1956: *United States Code,* Title 23, Section 127) and as amended by the Federal-Aid Highway Amendments of 1974 (P.L. 93-643, Section 106, January 4, 1975). The latter statute did not modify the 96-inch width limitation designated in the 1956 laws.

The contemporary prevalent maximum vehicle width specified in the state laws is 96 inches. Table 3.13 shows that there are 44 states with this particular width limitation. Six other states, moreover, maintain 102-inch restrictions and Hawaii alone permits a 108-inch width.

The trucking industry has consistently supported legislative proposals that would effectively increase vehicle width to 102 inches for two distinct reasons. First, an increase of six inches would definitely facilitate expanding the cubic capacity of cargo-carrying vehicles. Second, such legislative proposals would accommodate the transport of certain commodities possessing physical dimensions of multiples of eight feet.[13] This is presently impossible under the 96-inch width maximum due to the van wall construction. From the perspective of equipment design and operating conditions, supplemental width would provide numerous benefits, such as increased lateral stability, ameliorated steering and braking stability when cornering and under severe wind or emergency conditions, additional space for spring mountings and frame members for better spring systems, and additional space for larger tires and more tire and brake ventilation.[14]

Conversely, expansion in motor-truck width would conceivably affect several aspects of terminal facilities, namely existing driveways, alleys, ware-

TABLE 3.13

Maximum Vehicle Width Limits, by State, July 15, 1975

State	Width (inches)[a]	State	Width (inches)[a]
Alabama	96	Nebraska	96
Alaska	96	Nevada	96
Arizona	96[g]	New Hampshire	96
Arkansas	96	New Jersey	96[g]
California	96[c]	New Mexico	96[h]
Colorado	96[e]	New York	96[c]
Connecticut	102	North Carolina	96
Delaware	96	North Dakota	102[b,h]
Florida	96	Ohio	96[k]
Georgia	96[c]	Oklahoma	96[h]
Hawaii	108	Oregon	96[j]
Idaho	102[b]	Pennsylvania	96
Illinois	96[l]	Rhode Island	102
Indiana	96[c]	South Carolina	96[c]
Iowa	96	South Dakota	96
Kansas	96[c]	Tennessee	96
Kentucky	96[c]	Texas	96[c]
Louisiana	96	Utah	96
Maine	102[b]	Vermont	96
Maryland	96[c]	Virginia	96[c]
Massachusetts	96[c]	Washington	96
Michigan	96[c]	West Virginia	96[c]
Minnesota	96[f]	Wisconsin	96[d]
Mississippi	96	Wyoming	102[b]
Missouri	96[i]	District of Columbia	96
Montana	102[b]		

[a] Various exceptions for farm and construction equipment; public-utility vehicles; house trailers; urban, suburban, and school buses; haulage of agricultural and forest products; at wheels of vehicles for safety accessories, on designated highways, and as administratively authorized.

[b] On interstate highways, 96 inches.

[c] Urban buses, 102 inches.

[d] Urban buses, 104 inches. Interurban buses 102 inches on highways not part of the National Interstate and Defense Highway System.

[e] Buses and coaches, 102 inches.

[f] Urban buses, 108 inches.

[g] Vehicles in excess may be operated under special permit obtained in advance.

[h] On designated highways, 102 inches.

[i] Urban motor vehicles, 108 inches.

[j] Motor vehicle mobile homes, 14 feet on designated highways.

[k] Urban buses, 104 inches.

[l] Urban buses, 108 inches.

Source: Western Highway Institute, *State Motor Carriers Handbook: Sizes and Weights, Taxes and Fees* (Chicago: Commerce Clearing House, 1975), p. 1,012.

houses, and public alleys.[15] In addition, a majority of opponents of wider vehicles are against any enlargement of dimensions whatsoever and maintain primarily that larger vehicles can only come at the expense of decreased safety. John de Lorenzi of the American Automobile Association perhaps summed up this viewpoint in a 1974 statement before the Senate when he said:

> ". . . Gentlemen, we believe truck combinations are already too large. The passenger car operator, and our members in particular, intuitively fear sharing the same highway with such huge trucks. He hates to pass them because he can never be sure of what lies ahead until he moves into the opposing lane of traffic. (In rain or slush his windshield is invariably inundated beyond the capability of his wipers, restricting his forward vision and creating uncertainty as to safe passage.) He doesn't like to be followed by them, for just as often as not, they seem to be climbing up his rear bumper. When trucks occupy opposing lanes of traffic, the big rigs rock his vehicle as they pass only a few feet from him closing speeds of 100 mph or more sucking him into their wake. He doesn't like to follow them because they block his forward vision and his view of directional signs. They slow his travel speed uphill. . . ."[16]

The expansion of cubic capacity to be procured by an extra 6 inches would range between 6.4 and 6.5 percent.[17] However, the actual payload differential —productivity increase or decrease—would in effect depend upon cargo density. For high-density cargo there would be a reduction in maximum payload capacity because the wide vehicle would have a heavier tare weight. Commodities with a shipping density above 20.7 pounds per cubic foot would actually experience less capacity in a wider 40-foot trailer. But, as illustrated in Tables 3.11 and 3.12, all commodities below 19.1 pounds per cubic foot for 40-foot semitrailers with 102-inch width would experience an increase in maximum load capacity.[18]

In summary, width is predominantly uniform among the several states at 96 inches, the prescribed federal level for the interstate system, although 6 states maintain 102-inch width restrictions. The trucking industry in general would support a movement to 102-inch widths in order to expand cubic capacity by more than 6.5 percent for many commodities and to permit more efficient storage of 4- and 8-foot standard modular sizes of merchandise.

Height

The optimum motor-vehicle height limit is fundamentally a function of three factors: overhead clearances on highways, loading and unloading practices, and the effect of vehicle height on traffic.[19] Heights are relatively uniform

TABLE 3.14

Maximum Vehicle Height Limits, by State, July 15, 1975

State	Height (feet, inches)	State	Height (feet, inches)
Alabama	13, 6	Montana	13, 6
Alaska	13, 6	Nebraska	13, 6[k]
Arizona	13, 6	Nevada	14, 0
Arkansas	13, 6	New Hampshire	13, 6
California	13, 6[e]	New Jersey	13, 6[c]
Colorado	13, 6[a]	New Mexico	13, 6
Connecticut	13, 6[f]	New York	13, 6
Delaware	13, 6	North Carolina	13, 6
Florida	13, 6	North Dakota	13, 6
Georgia	13, 6	Ohio	13, 6
Hawaii	13, 6	Oklahoma	13, 6
Idaho	14, 0	Oregon	13, 6[h]
Illinois	13, 6	Pennsylvania	13, 6[d]
Indiana	13, 6	Rhode Island	13, 6
Iowa	13, 6	South Carolina	13, 6
Kansas	13, 6	South Dakota	13, 6
Kentucky	13, 6[g]	Tennessee	13, 6
Louisiana	13, 6	Texas	13, 6
Maine	13, 6[b]	Utah	14, 0
Maryland	13, 6	Vermont	13, 6
Massachusetts	13, 6	Virginia	13, 6
Michigan	13, 6	Washington	13, 6[h]
Minnesota	13, 6	West Virginia	12, 6[i]
Mississippi	13, 6	Wisconsin	13, 6
Missouri	13, 6[j]	Wyoming	14, 0
		District of Columbia	12, 6

[a] On designated highways; 12 feet, 6 inches on other highways.

[b] Including load 14 feet; various exceptions for vehicles hauling forest products and construction materials.

[c] Vehicles in excess may be operated under special permit obtained in advance.

[d] Motor bus in municipal corporations, 14 feet, 6 inches; other buses 12 feet, 6 inches.

[e] Boom or mast of a forklift truck, 14 feet.

[f] Not applicable to loads of hay or straw.

[g] On designated highways; 11 feet, 6 inches on other highways.

[h] Auto transports, 14 feet.

[i] Auto transports, 13 feet, 6 inches; any vehicle on designated highways, 13 feet, 6 inches.

[j] Urban vehicles, 15 feet.

[k] Vehicles moving unbaled livestock forage, 18 feet.

Source: Western Highway Institute, *State Moror Carriers Handbook; Sizes and Weights, Taxes and Fees* (Chicago: Commerce Clearing House, 1975), p. 1,012.

throughout the United States, as illustrated in Table 3.14. Forty-six states presently maintain a physical limitation of 13.5 feet; two states are below this at 12.5 feet, whereas four states have a maximum of 14.0 feet. Relative to overhead structures, those which would not clear vehicles of 13.5 feet are declining annually as older highways are rebuilt to meet newer design standards. This factor, when coupled with the present limit of 13.5 feet or higher in 49 states, indicates that no major physical obstacle exists to restrict vehicles of 13.5 feet on the domestic highway system.[20] Data in Table 3.15 elucidates the potential consequences of increasing the maximum height limit by illustrating the small number of structures with less than 14-foot clearance on the interstate system and on principal state highways in 1961.

The loading and unloading dilemma is realistically a question of whether or not a greater height could be adequately utilized. The important considerations are essentially the amount of labor involved, the difficulty of maneuvering the right type of mechanical lifter to take advantage of additional height, and the fact that certain commodities can only be stacked to certain levels because they sustain damage from their own weight if stacked higher. Consensus regarding an observation that only a few commodities comprising a minute percentage of total highway movement would positively benefit from increased height and higher legal limits for this sole purpose is difficult to justify.[21]

Last, although a vehicle's overturning propensity would be expanded if vehicle height were extended without a simultaneous proportional increase in width, the height of a vehicle, within practical bounds, has an inconsequential effect upon traffic safety or the operation of other vehicles.[22] Vehicle height in most states is fixed at 13.5 feet. Albeit additional height could be physically accommodated within the present system, the trucking industry in general has demonstrated only minute interest in obtaining an increase for the simple

TABLE 3.15

Vertical Clearance of Structures, 1961

Highway System	Number of Miles	Number of Structures	Number of Structures below 14 Feet	Percent
Interstate	40,560	22,259	158	.710
Principle state*	250,400	71,003	1,169	1.646
Total	290,960	93,262	1,327	2.356

*Excludes interstate routes.
Note: Includes bridges, overpasses, underpasses, and tunnels.
Source: U.S., Congress, House, *Maximum Desirable Dimensions and Weights of Vehicles Operated on the Federal-Aid Systems,* 88th Cong., 2d sess., H. Doc. 354, 1964, pp. 91-92.

reason that only relatively few commodities would benefit. Motor-vehicle lengths are of much more significant interest to the trucking industry.

Length

Overall vehicle length together with axle weights are extolled as the two most critical factors in the total public-policy problem of arriving at the optimal dimensions and weights of motor vehicles.[23] Length is economically beneficial in two respects: not only is cubic capacity expanded, but by incorporating additional axles, additional length facilitates higher gross loads without increasing axle-weight restrictions. In this regard, Table 3.16 illustrates the maximum lengths for single-unit trucks, semitrailers, truck-tractor and semitrailer, and other combinations. Table 3.17 summarizes the information contained in Table 3.16 and cogently demonstrates the present disparity existing among states with respect to length maximums.

Single-Unit Trucks

Table 3.17 shows the difference in permissible lengths of single-unit trucks as of July 15, 1975. Thirty-three states, moreover, permit lengths of 40 feet or more. Also, 17 states specify 35 feet as a maximum while 1 state imposes a legal restriction of 36 feet. The U.S. average permitted length for single-unit trucks in 1975 was 39.7 feet. This average length compares with 38.3 feet reported in a 1964 study (using 1963 data) and generally supports a comprehensive conclusion therein that single-unit truck lengths have remained fairly stable in recent years due primarily to the declining importance of the single-unit truck in over-the-road operation.[24]

Semitrailer or Trailer

Table 3.17 discloses that only 11 states (21.7 percent) explicitly declare length maximums for semitrailers or trailers. Of those states specified, the range is 35 to 55 feet, with an average of 41.8 feet. Of the remaining 40 states, 34 have no restriction and 6 make no specification.

Truck-Tractor Semitrailer

Table 3.17 reveals that 30 states presently maintain a 55-foot limitation on truck-tractor semitrailers. However, 20 states maintain restrictions in excess of 55 feet, with 7 states at 60 feet and 10 states at 65. The U.S. average permitted for truck-tractor semitrailers in 1975 was 58.4 feet, an increase from 54.7 feet in 1963.[25]

Other Combinations

In addition to the truck-tractor semitrailer mentioned above, there are two types of trailer combinations: one combination consists of two units, a truck and full trailer; the other is comprised of three units, a truck-tractor semitrailer and full trailer. In the latter combination, both trailers are frequently identical inasmuch as the full trailer is assembled by a converted dolly located under the front of the semitrailer.[26] Thus assembled, these units are referred to as twin trailers or "double bottoms." Yet, operating twin trailers is currently prohibited or seriously restricted in many states. Table 3.17 reflects the fact that two lengths dominate the laws of the several states for other combinations. At present, 17 states permit 55-foot combinations, whereas 22 states maintain a 65-foot limitation. Of the remaining states, 9 are in the range of 50 to 75 feet, and 3 states do not permit other combinations. For the 48 states that respectively sanction other combinations, the mean length during calendar year 1975 was 61.5 feet. This particular category has also gained significantly since 1963, when the average was just 56 feet.[27]

The three salient factors of motor-vehicle length relative to desirable operations in both the traffic stream and optimal cargo handling are essentially the length of the vehicle with regard to loading and unloading at dock and warehouse facilities, the length of the vehicle with respect to horizontal turns and curves (off-tracking operating characteristics), and the effect of vehicle length on the traffic stream.[28] An intense debate does not necessarily surround the first two factors since single-unit trucks beyond 40 feet in length are not only difficult to maneuver, but likewise are not optimally desired for use in present terminal facilities. Furthermore, little need has been indicated for a single cargo unit in excess of 40 feet.[29] The desirable length for combination units ultimately centers on the potential trade-off between increase in carrier productivity and operational safety. Off-tracking characteristics of any truck or combination are a dual function of length and configuration of the articulated vehicle and can be readily computed. For example, a 65-foot-long double bottom has better off-tracking characteristics (less demand of space) than a 55-foot-long truck-tractor semitrailer.[30]

Although the 40-foot trailer is basically the industry standard, combinations with two 27-foot cargo bodies (twin trailers) are in much greater demand by the motor-carrier industry because of their fundamental economy in line-haul operation, flexibility in terminal operations, and convenience and economy in the urban distribution of cargo.[31] However, as evidenced in Table 3.18, 16 states prohibit entirely the movement of twin trailers on their highway

TABLE 3.16

Maximum Vehicle Length Limits, by State, July 15, 1975 (in feet)

State	Single-Unit Truck	Single-Unit Semitrailer or Trailer	Truck-Tractor Semitrailer	Other Combination
Alabama	40	NS	55	NP
Alaska	40	40	60	65
Arizona	40	NS	65	65
Arkansas	40	NS	55	65
California	40	40	65	65
Colorado	35	NR	65[b]	65[b]
Connecticut	55	NR[t]	55	NP
Delaware	40	40	55[e]	65
Florida	35[c]	NS[d]	55	55
Georgia	55	NR	55[r]	55[r]
Hawaii	40	NR	55	65
Idaho	40	NR	65	75[f]
Illinois	42	45	55[g]	60[h]
Indiana	36	NR	55[i]	65
Iowa	35	NR[a]	55[k]	55[k]
Kansas	42.5	NS[m]	60[l]	65
Kentucky	35[cc]	NR	55[aa]	65
Louisiana	35	NR	60	65
Maine	45	45	56.5	56.5
Maryland	40	55	55[n]	65[o]
Massachusetts	35	NR	55	NP
Michigan	40	NR	55[p]	65[dd]
Minnesota	40	NR	55[q]	55[q]
Mississippi	35	NR	55	65
Missouri	40	NR	55[r]	60[s]
Montana	40	NR	60	65
Nebraska	40	NR[t]	60[e]	75
Nevada	40	NR	75	55[u]
New Hampshire	35	NR	55[n]	55
New Jersey	35	NR[a]	55	65
New Mexico	40	NR	65	55
New York	35	NR[a]	55[r]	55[r]
North Carolina	35[bb]	NR	55	55
North Dakota	40[j]	NR	65	65
Ohio	40	NR	55	65
Oklahoma	40	NR	65	65
Oregon	35	35	60	75
Pennsylvania	35	NR	55[r]	55[o,r]
Rhode Island	40	40	55	55
South Carolina	40[j]	NR	55	55[v]
South Dakota	35	NR	60	60

	Single-Unit			
State	Truck	Semitrailer or Trailer	Truck-Tractor Semitrailer	Other Combination
Tennessee	40	NR	55	55
Texas	45	NR	65	65[ee]
Utah	45	45	65	65
Vermont	55	NS	55[n]	55
Virginia	40	NR	55	55
Washington	35	40	65	65[w]
West Virginia	35	NR	50[x]	50[x]
Wisconsin	35	35[y]	55[z]	55
Wyoming	50	NR	75	75
District of Columbia	40	NR	55	55

[a]Trailer, 35 feet.

[b]Combinations may use up to 65 feet on designated highways.

[c]Three or more axles, 40 feet.

[d]Two-axle trailer, 35 feet; three-axle trailer, 40 feet.

[e]Auto transports, 65 feet.

[f]Three- or four-unit combinations, 98 feet on designated highways.

[g]Auto transports on four-lane and designated highways, 65 feet.

[h]Certain vehicles on four-lane and designated highways, 65 feet.

[i]Auto transports and trucks pulling house trailers, 60 feet.

[j]For three-axle vehicles; less than three-axles, 35 feet.

[k]Auto and boat transports and three-unit combination permitted 60 feet.

[l]Auto and boat transports, 60 feet.

[m]Applies only to trailers.

[n]Excluding overhang of auto transports.

[o]Exception for articles impossible to dismember, permitted 70 feet.

[p]Auto transports, 63 feet.

[q]Not applicable to certain objects transported by a public utility.

[r]Auto transports, 60 feet, including load.

[s]On state primary highways and on interstate routes; 55 feet on other roads.

[t]Trailer, 40 feet.

[u]Subject to rules of the Department of Highways, 105 feet.

[v]Certain vehicles in daylight hours, 60 feet.

[w]Stinger-steered semitrailer combination, 70 feet with load.

[x]On designated highways, 55 feet.

[y]Semitrailer measured from rear thereof to rear of vehicle to which attached.

[z]Auto transports allowed up to 10 feet additional on Class A highways by annual permit.

[aa]On designated highways; 30 feet on others.

[bb]For two-axle vehicles.

[cc]On designated highways; 26.5 feet on others.

[dd]Combination of truck-tractor, semitrailer, and trailer on designated highways, 65 feet.

[ee]No mobile home and vehicle combination may exceed a total length of 55 feet.

Note: NP = not permitted; NR = not restricted; NS = not specified. Various exceptions for utility vehicles and loads; house trailers; mobile homes; and urban, suburban, and school buses.

Source: Western Highway Institute, *State Motor Carrier's Handbook: Size and Weights, Taxes and Fees* (Chicago: Commerce Clearing House, 1975), p. 1,012.

TABLE 3.17

Maximum Vehicle Length Limits, Summary, July 15, 1975

Length (in feet)	Number of States Permitting Indicated Vehicle Lengths							
	Single-unit Truck	Percent	Semitrailer or Trailer	Percent	Truck-tractor Semitrailer	Percent	Other Combinations	Percent
35	17	33.33	2	3.92	*	—	—	—
36	1	1.96	—	—	—	—	—	—
40	24	47.07	5	9.81	—	—	—	—
42	1	1.96	—	—	—	—	—	—
42.5	1	1.96	—	—	—	—	—	—
45	3	5.88	3	5.88	1	1.96	—	—
50	1	1.96	—	—	—	—	1	1.96
55	3	5.88	1	1.96	30	58.82	17	33.33
56.5	—	—	—	—	1	1.96	1	1.96
60	—	—	—	—	7	13.73	3	5.88
65	—	—	—	—	10	19.61	22	43.14
75	—	—	—	—	2	3.92	4	7.85
NR	—	—	34	66.67	—	—	—	—
NS	—	—	6	11.76	—	—	—	—
NP	—	—	—	—	—	—	3	5.88
Total	51	100	51	100	51	100	51	100

*Dashes indicate none in category.

Note: NR = not restricted; NS = not specified; NP = not permitted.

Source: Compiled by the authors.

networks.* In addition, only twin trailers at less-economic lengths of 55 feet and 60 feet can be operated in another three states and one state, respectively.

The impact of vehicle length upon the traffic stream is a somewhat moot point. The paramount consideration to opponents of longer vehicles is the question of operating safety. As one example of the type of disagreement that exists, one individual has stated his opposition to any length increase because it is likely that some parts of the National System of Interstate and Defense Highways cannot safely accommodate trucks longer than 50 to 55 feet even though the system was designed and built to high engineering standards.[32] On the other hand, Robley Winfrey and his associates discovered that lengths up to 100 feet are desirable on the interstate system.[33] Similar disparities exist for passing, width of pavements, and braking distances, with each party citing the study that best supports its own particular viewpoint.

MOTOR VEHICLE WEIGHTS

The fundamental difference between the effects of weights and of dimensions is that weight primarily influences the serviceability and life of the pavement and structures by imposing stress upon them, that is, overstressing diminishes serviceability and accelerates the reconstruction and/or replacement process. On the other hand, vehicle dimensions enjoy a more prominent role in highway traffic operations and can in turn affect the general behavior of vehicles in the traffic stream.[34] Motor-vehicle weight may be classified as axle weight, which may be subclassified into single- and tandem-axle weight, and gross vehicle weight. Both are subject to indirect federal control and direct state control.

Increasing permissible gross weights and axle weights would enable motor carriers to transport more per load of those heavy commodities that presently fail to cube out. Again, density becomes the predominant factor but in this situation the heavy commodities stand to profit through additional weight. Table 3.19 illustrates the selected densities of some typical commodities hauled by motor carriers. As noted, the commodities of 12 pounds per cubic foot and under are considered to be light and bulky goods, and will hence cube out before existing load limits are attained; the category of 17 to 22 pounds per cubic foot is illustrative of the optimum weight range for commodities; and a

---

*These are Alabama, Connecticut, Florida, Maine, Massachusetts, New Hampshire, North Carolina, Pennsylvania, Rhode Island, South Carolina, Tennessee, Vermont, Virginia, West Virginia, Wisconsin, and the District of Columbia.

TABLE 3.18

Current Status of Twin Trailers in the United States, December 31, 1975

Length in Feet	Number of States	Percentage
65 or over	31	61
60	1	2
55	3	6
NP	16	31
Total	51	100

Note: NP = not permitted.

Source: "What is the Status of Truck Size-Weights?," *Traffic World* 165 (February 16, 1976): 37.

TABLE 3.19

Densities of Typical Commodities Handled by Motor Carriers

Commodity	Density in Pounds per Cubic Foot
Mattresses and box springs	4.0
Blankets	4.0–6.0
Steel lavatories	7.6
Mufflers	8.9
Rubber hose	9.9
Washing machines	10.4
Copying machines	11.1
Air cleaners; dehumidifiers	11.3
Solid tires	18.0
Crib springs	19.8
Frozen cream	20.0+
Solid rubber toys	21.5
Rolled cereals (Ralstons)	21.7
Canned or bottled soft drinks	40.0
Coca Cola syrup (in 10 gallon kegs)	43.4
Bulk automotive gasoline	46.1
Cooked, cured, or preserved meats	52.0
Tobacco, in wooden boxes	59.0
Electric flashlight batteries	60.0
Paint, lacquers	62.0–70.0
Bulk milk	63.0
Spark plugs	64.0

Source: U.S. Department of Transportation, Federal Highway Administration, "Effects of Increasing Truck Size and Weight on Increase in Freight Handling Capacity per Truck Unit," mimeographed draft (1975).

density greater than 25 pounds per cubic foot represents heavy commodities. This last group contains commodities that could take advantage of more liberal weights.

Unlike motor-vehicle dimensions, there is less polemics regarding the percentage of highway haulage that could possibly profit from higher weights. Table 3.10 indicated that over 90 percent of the tonnage moved in 1963 was in the heavy-commodity classification and could, thus, theoretically capitalize from a weight-liberalization law. In a later study, Winfrey and his associates basically concurred with this finding by contending that the bulk of goods transported over highways has densities such that the legal axle-weight limits are attained before the cargo body cubes out.[35] The importance of weight in general has also been substantiated in the size and weight legislation in recent years. That is to say, the trucking industry, until fairly recently, has always inordinately emphasized the weight factors. From yet another perspective, Table 3.20 reveals the result of a recent Federal Highway Administration compilation, which estimates that only 4.49 percent of all trucks and 58 percent of combination trucks could augment shipping capacity as a result of P.L. 93-643.[36] Even though the number and percentages of vehicles appear

TABLE 3.20

Estimated Number of Trucks which Will Have Increased Shipping Capacity as a Result of P.L. 93-643, 1975

Type of Vehicle	Registered Gross Vehicle Weight	Type of Benefit	Number
Single-unit trucks[a]	32,000–39,000	axle	39,600
Single-unit trucks	40,000+	axle	330,860
Combination vehicles			
Semitrailer, three axle	50,000+	axle	25,630
Semitrailer, four axle	60,000+	axle	158,440
Full trailer, four axle	50,000+	axle	16,310
Semitrailer, five axle	60,000+	g.v.w.[b]	272,610
Full trailer, five axle	60,000+	g.v.w.	16,310
Full trailer, six axle	60,000+	g.v.w.	9,320
Semitrailer and full trailer	60,000+	g.v.w.	177,080
Total	—[c]	—	1,046,160

[a] All single-unit vehicles below 31,999 gross vehicle weight were omitted.

[b] g.v.w. = gross vehicle weight.

[c] not applicable.

Source: U.S., Department of Transportation, Federal Highway Administration, "Effects of Increasing Truck Size and Weight on Increase in Freight Handling Capacity Per Truck Unit," mimeographed draft (1975), Table 3.

small, the FHWA has failed to indicate the proportion of freightage transported by this group. However, this does not appear entirely unreasonable inasmuch as almost 90 percent of the loads carried on main rural roads moved via various truck combinations.

Gross Vehicle Weight

Gross vehicle weight does not affect pavement design. Since the design factor is primarily predicated upon axle weights, axle spacing, and the number of axle applications, a truck's practical gross weight equals the sum of the maximum limits of the axles.[37] Increased gross weight can, however, adversely affect bridges, particularly if the wheel base is not long enough to properly distribute the weight.[38]

The Federal-Aid Highway Amendments of 1974 provided that those states which were restricted on the federal-aid interstate highway system by P.L. 84-627 to axle and gross weights less than those set forth in the new law, could increase their weights to the new maximum limits of 20,000 pounds for a single axle, 34,000 pounds for a tandem axle, and a gross vehicle weight of 80,000 pounds (including all tolerances). The new law was permissive because each respective state could decide for itself whether to adopt the new weights or retain the present restrictions. Table 3.21 reveals the individual state maximum gross weight restrictions before and after the enactment of P.L. 93-643 for both the interstate and noninterstate systems. Table 3.22 summarizes the data presented in Table 3.21 and depicts more realistically the dissimilarity that pervades the legal statutes of the several states. On the interstate system, 16 states (32 percent) are restricted to 73,000 to 73,280 pounds maximum gross vehicle weight; 21 states have limitations between 73,281 and 80,000 pounds; and another 13 states exceed 80,000 pounds, with 7 of these states surpassing 100,000 pounds.

The noninterstate disaggregation by weight is supportive of an earlier proposition advanced in Chapter 2, which stated in effect that the interstate system, generally constructed to the highest standards, was restricted to vehicles lighter than those tolerated on other roads. Although the lower weight classifications (below 80,000 pounds) of noninterstate correspond almost exactly to the interstate categories, there are 27 states (52.9 percent) in the noninterstate group that have limitations of about 80,000 pounds, and 16 of these states have regulations beyond 100,000 pounds.

Several other considerations regarding gross vehicle weight should be examined. On the positive side, higher gross weight translates into approximately 7.7 to 11.9 percent improvement in fuel utilization, depending on vehicle type and operation. The variation in consumption is attributable to the great degree of difference in tare weights and legally permissible weight maxi-

TABLE 3.21

Effects of P.L. 93–643 on State Maximum Gross Weight Limits, October 10, 1975

State	Interstate		Noninterstate	
	Before	After	Before	After
Alabama	73,280	80,000	73,280	92,400
Alaska	—	—	114,000	114,000
Arizona	76,800	80,000	76,800	80,000
Arkansas	73,280	73,280	73,280	73,280
California	79,100	80,000	79,100	80,000
Colorado	76,800	80,000	85,000	85,000
Connecticut	73,000	73,000	73,000	73,000
Delaware	73,280	73,280	73,280	73,280
Florida	73,271	80,000	138,271*	138,271*
	—	—	73,271	80,000
Georgia	73,280	80,000	73,280	80,000
Hawaii	80,800	80,800	80,800	80,800
Idaho	105,500*	105,500*	105,500*	105,500*
	76,800	76,800	76,800	76,800
Illinois	73,280	73,280	73,280	73,280
Indiana	—	—	—	127,400*
	73,280	73,280	73,280	73,280
Iowa	73,280	73,280	73,280	73,280
Kansas	—	—	130,000*	130,000*
	73,280	80,000	85,500	85,500
Kentucky	73,280	80,000	82,000	82,000
Louisiana	73,280	80,000	73,280	80,000
Maine	73,280	80,000	73,280	80,000
Maryland	73,280	73,280	73,280	73,280
Massachusetts	—	—	127,400*	127,400*
	73,000	80,000	73,000	80,000
Michigan	136,000	136,000	136,000	136,000
Minnesota	73,280	73,280	73,280	73,280
Mississippi	73,280	73,280	73,280	73,280
Missouri	73,280	73,280	73,280	73,280
Montana	105,500*	105,500*	105,500	105,500
	76,800	76,800	—	—
Nebraska	95,000*	95,000*	95,000	95,000
	71,146	71,146	—	—
Nevada	129,000*	129,000*	129,000*	129,000*
	76,800	80,000	76,800	109,000
New Hampshire	73,280	73,280	73,280	73,280
New Jersey	73,280	80,850	73,280	80,850
New Mexico	86,400	86,400	86,400	86,400
New York	73,280	80,000*	127,400*	127,400*
		73,280	80,000	
North Carolina	73,280	79,800	79,800	79,800

(continued)

65

(Table 3.21 continued)

State	Interstate		Noninterstate	
	Before	After	Before	After
North Dakota	73,280	80,000	82,000	105,500
Ohio	78,000	80,000	80,000	80,000
Oklahoma	73,280	80,000	90,000	90,000
Oregon	105,500	105,500	105,500	105,500
Pennsylvania	73,280	73,280	73,280	73,280
Rhode Island	88,000	88,000	88,000	88,000
South Carolina	80,608	80,608	80,608	80,608
South Dakota	73,280	80,000	95,000	95,000
Tennessee	73,280	73,280	73,280	73,280
Texas	72,000	80,000	72,000	80,000
Utah	105,500*	105,500*	105,500*	105,500*
	87,890	87,890	87,890	87,890
Vermont	73,280	73,280	73,280	73,280
Virginia	73,280	79,800	79,800	79,800
Washington	105,500*	105,500*	105,500*	105,500*
	76,000	76,000	76,000	76,000
West Virginia	73,280	80,000	73,280	80,000
Wisconsin	73,000	73,000	73,000	73,000
Wyoming	73,950	80,000	101,000	101,000
District of Columbia	73,280	73,280	73,280	73,280

*On designated highways.

Note: Including tolerances grandfathered by previous laws and laws passed with later effective dates.

Sources: Western Highway Institute, "Effects of the Federal-Aid Highway Amendments of 1974 on State Axle and Gross Weight Limits as of November 1, 1975," Research Summary Series, no. 1–75 (n.p., October 17, 1975); "Maximum State Vehicle Size-Weight Limits," *Traffic World* 165 (February 16, 1976): 38–39; "State Legal Maximum Dimensions and Weights of Motor Vehicles Compared with AASHTO Standards," prepared by the American Association of State Highway and Transportation Officials (n.p., December 31, 1974); Ibid., December 31, 1975.

mums for each vehicle type.[39] Another possible benefit can be derived from the assumption that increased gross weight will ultimately reduce the number of freight vehicles in the traffic stream.[40] This would mean a smaller exposure to the frequency of accidents and thus, theoretically, fewer highway-related deaths. To offset these gains, however, the opposition cites numerous safety considerations, such as the need for higher brake standards, improved acceleration and hill climbing, superior coupling devices and jackknife control, more sophisticated underride guards, and better control of splash and spray tendencies.[41]

TABLE 3.22

State Maximum Gross Weight Limits, Summary, October 10, 1975

Limit, in Pounds	Number of States			
	Interstate	Percent	Noninterstate	Percent
73,000	2	4.0	2	3.9
73,380	14	28.0	13	25.5
73,281–79,999	2	4.0	2	3.9
80,000	19	38.0	7	13.7
80,001–89,999	5	10.0	7	13.7
90,000–99,999	1	2.0	4	7.8
100,000+	7	14.0	17	31.5
Total	50	100	51	100

Note: Excludes Alaska.
Source: Compiled by the authors.

Axle Weights

The functional relationship existing between axle loadings and pavement life has been well established through such empirical investigations as Road Test One-Maryland, the WASHO Road Test, and the AASHO Road Test. The maximum allowable axle weight represents the most critical limitation in both highway utilization and in truck operations. For the highway, the magnitude of the axle weight together with the axle spacing and the frequency of application determine the expected life of highway surfaces and bridges.* With respect to vehicle operation, the legally permissible axle weights play a principle role both individually and collectively in establishing the payloads of freight that can be transported by particular classes of vehicles.[42]

Table 3.23 illustrates the respective state maximum single- and tandem-axle weight laws before and after the passage of P.L. 93-643 for both interstate and noninterstate systems. Table 3.24 is a recapitulation of the data presented in Table 3.23 and additionally discloses the inequality that permeates the state

---

*Higher axle weights reduce the expected pavement life and this diminishment of pavement life is usually expressed in terms of increased annual maintenance costs of pavement overlays. It is the process of translating the lessening of pavement life to increased annual costs that critics attack as unreliable.

TABLE 3.23

Effects of P.L. 93–643 on State Maximum Axle Weight Limits, October 10, 1975

State	Interstate Before		Interstate After		Noninterstate Before		Noninterstate After	
	Single Axle	Tandem Axle	Single Axle	Tandem Axle	Single Axle	Tandem Axle	Single Axle	Tandem Axle
Alabama	19,800	39,600	20,000	39,600	19,800	39,600	22,000	44,000
Alaska	—	—	20,000	—	20,000	34,000	20,000	34,000
Arizona	18,000	32,000	20,000	34,000	18,000	32,000	20,000	34,000
Arkansas	18,000	32,000	18,000	32,000	18,000	32,000	18,000	32,000
California	18,000	32,000	20,000	34,000	18,000	32,000	20,000	24,000
Colorado	18,000	36,000	20,000	36,000	18,000	36,000	18,000	36,000
Connecticut	22,848	36,720	22,848	36,720	22,848	36,720	22,848	36,720
Delaware	20,000	36,000	20,000	36,000	20,000	36,000	20,000	36,000
Florida	22,000	44,000	22,000	44,000	22,000	44,000	22,000	44,000
Georgia	20,340	40,680	20,340	40,680	20,340	40,680	20,340	40,680
Hawaii	24,000	32,000	24,000	32,000	24,000	32,000	24,000	32,000
Idaho	20,000	34,000	20,000	34,000	20,000	34,000	20,000	34,000
Illinois	18,000	32,000	18,000	32,000	18,000	32,000	18,000	32,000
Indiana	18,000	32,000	18,000	32,000	18,000	32,000	18,000	32,000
Iowa	18,540	32,960	18,540	32,960	18,540	32,960	18,540	32,960
Kansas	18,000	32,000	20,000	34,000	20,000	34,000	20,000	34,000
Kentucky	18,900	33,600	20,000	34,000	21,000	35,700	21,000	35,700
Louisiana	18,000	32,000	20,000	34,000	18,000	32,000	20,000	34,000
Maine	22,000	32,000	22,000	34,000	22,000	42,000	22,000	38,000
Maryland	22,400	40,000	22,400	40,000	22,400	41,000	22,400	41,000
Massachusetts	22,400	36,000	22,400	36,000	22,400	36,000	22,400	36,000
Michigan	18,000	32,000	18,000	32,000	18,000	32,000	18,000	32,000
Minnesota	18,000	32,000	18,000	32,000	18,000	32,000	18,000	32,000

State						
Mississippi	18,000	32,000	18,000	32,000	18,000	32,000
Missouri	18,000	32,000	18,000	32,000	18,000	32,000
Montana	20,000	34,000	20,000	34,000	20,000	34,000
Nebraska	20,000	34,000	20,000	34,000	20,000·	34,000
Nevada	20,000	34,000	20,000	34,000	20,000	34,000
New Hampshire	22,400	36,000	22,400	36,000	22,400	36,000
New Jersey	22,520	33,600	23,520	34,000	23,520	35,700
New Mexico	21,600	34,320	21,600	34,320	21,600	34,320
New York	22,400	36,000	22,400	36,000	22,400	36,000
North Carolina	19,000	36,000	20,000	36,000	20,000	38,000
North Dakota	18,000	32,000	20,000	34,000	20,000	34,000
Ohio	19,380	32,960	20,000	34,000	20,000	34,000
Oklahoma	18,000	32,000	20,000	34,000	20,000	34,000
Oregon	20,000	34,000	20,000	34,000	20,000	34,000
Pennsylvania	23,070	37,080	23,070	37,080	23,070	37,080
Rhode Island	22,400	36,000	22,400	36,000	22,400	36,000
South Carolina	22,000	36,000	22,000	36,000	22,000	39,600
South Dakota	18,000	32,000	20,000	34,000	20,000	34,000
Tennessee	18,000	32,000	18,000	32,000	18,000	32,000
Texas	18,000	32,000	20,000	34,000	20,000	34,000
Utah	20,000	36,000	20,000	36,000	20,000	36,000
Vermont	22,400	36,000	22,400	36,000	22,400	36,000
Virginia	18,900	33,600	20,000	35,700	21,000	35,700
Washington	20,000	34,000	20,000	34,000	20,000	34,000
West Virginia	18,900	33,600	20,000	34,000	18,900	34,000
Wisconsin	19,500	32,000	19,500	32,000	19,500	32,000
Wyoming	20,000	36,000	20,000	36,000	20,000	36,000
District of Columbia	18,000	32,000	18,000	32,000	22,000	38,000

Note: Includes tolerances grandfathered by previous laws and laws passed with later effective dates. Dashes indicate category not applicable.

Sources: Western Highway Institute, "Effects of the Federal-Aid Highway Amendments of 1974 on State Axle and Gross Weight Limits as of November 1, 1975," Research Summary Series, no. 1–75 (n.p., October 17, 1975): "State Legal Maximum Dimensions and Weights of Motor Vehicles Compared with AASHTO Standards," prepared by the American Association of State Highway and Transportation Officials (n.p., December 31, 1975).

TABLE 3.24

State Maximum Axle Weight Limits, Summary, October 10, 1975

Limit, in Pounds	Interstate		Noninterstate	
	Number of States	Percent	Number of States	Percent
18,000	9	18.0	9	17.6
18,001–19,999	2	4.0	2	3.9
20,000	24	48.0	21	41.2
20,001–22,399	5	10.0	9	17.6
22,400	6	12.0	6	11.8
22,401 +	4	8.0	4	7.9
Total	50	100	51	100

Limit, in Pounds	Interstate		Noninterstate	
	Number of States	Percent	Number of States	Percent
32,000	11	22.0	10	19.6
32,001–33,999	1	2.0	1	2.0
34,000	20	40.0	17	33.3
34,001–35,999	1	2.0	4	7.9
36,000	11	22.0	9	17.6
36,001 +	6	12.0	10	19.6
Total	50	100	51	100

Note: Excludes Alaska.
Source: Compiled by the authors.

TABLE 3.25

Number of Permits by Oversize Class, 1966

Type of Permit	Number Issued	Percent of Class
Overlength	157,655	7.80
Overwidth	607,724	30.08
Overheight	21,126	1.05
Overlength and overwidth	851,916	42.16
Overlength and overheight	10,026	.50
Overwidth and overheight	137,990	6.83
Overlength, overwidth, and overheight	232,108	11.48
Not specified	1,994	.10
Total	2,020,539	100.00

Source: Roy Jorgensen et. al., *Oversize-Overwieght Permit Operation on State Highways*, National Cooperative Highway Research Program Report 80 (Washington, D.C.: National Academy of Sciences, National Academy of Engineering, 1969), p. 19.

TABLE 3.26

Number of Permits by Overweight Class, 1966

Type of Permit	Number Issued	Percent of Class
Gross weight	178,458	25.49
Axle	21,325	3.05
Gross weight and axle	440,494	62.91
Unknown	59,926	8.55
Total	700,203	100.00

Source: Roy Jorgensen et. al., *Oversize-Overwieght Permit Operation on State Highways*, National Cooperative Highway Research Program Report 80 (Washington, D.C.: National Academy of Sciences, National Academy of Engineering, 1969), p. 19.

and federal systems relative to single- and tandem-axle weights. Indeed, single-axle limits on the interstate system range from 18,000 to 24,000 pounds because of the grandfather provisions. The most predominant weight is the current restriction imposed by P.L. 93-643 of 20,000 pounds, with 24 states allowing this limit. However, 11 states have lower legal restrictions, whereas

15 states exceed 20,000 pounds. On the noninterstate highway network, there is little difference in absolute numbers, with the exception of the 20,001- to 22,399-pound grouping. This particular classification demonstrates a net gain of three states at the expense of the 20,000-pound category.

For the tandem axles, the legal restrictions range from 32,000 to 44,000 pounds for both interstate and noninterstate highways. Again, the most recurrent weight is the 34,000 pounds presently specified by P.L. 93-643. But, two other weights occur frequently in the statutes of the several states. These weights are 32,000 and 36,000 pounds. On both the interstate and noninterstate systems ten states retain the tandem-axle weights originally designated in 1956; eleven and nine states, respectively, have 36,000-pound restrictions. From an overall viewpoint, on the interstate network 18 states permit limits in excess of 34,000 pounds, while 23 states do so on noninterstate roadways.

OVERSIZE-OVERWEIGHT PERMIT OPERATION ON STATE HIGHWAYS

There are certain instances when it is necessary to transport freight at sizes and/or weights surpassing the legal limitations of the several states. The major users of these permits in 1966 were the construction and mobile-home industries, followed closely by the aerospace, agriculture, forest, boating, mining, oil and gas, and public-power industries, and the military.[43] Tables 3.25 and 3.26 display the number of permits issued in 1966 by oversize class and by overweight class. Several observations can be gleaned from these two tables. First, oversize permits outnumber overweight permits by about 3 to 1; second, within the oversize class, over 90 percent of the permits issued involved width, 61.94 percent were concerned with length, and only 19.86 percent were issued for overheight. With respect to overweight permits, the majority exceeded both gross- and axle-weight limitations. Unfortunately, the laws, regulations, and procedures governing the issuance of these special permits are even more varied than the size and weight limits themselves.

NOTES

1. See John W. Fuller III, "Current Issues in the Regulation of Motor Vehicle Sizes and Weights" (Ph.D. diss., reprinted in U. S., Congress, *Congressional Record,* 90th Cong., 2d sess., July 24, 1968, 114, pt. 18: 23,178–80.

2. Ibid., p. 23,180.

3. See Bureau of Economics, Interstate Commerce Commission, *Transport Economics* 1, no. 4 (1974): p. 4.

4. *1975 Motor Truck Facts* (New York: Motor Vehicle Manufacturers Association of the United States, 1975), p. 37, n. 1.

5. U.S., Department of Transportation, Federal Highway Administration, *Highway Statistics, 1973* (Washington, D.C.: Government Printing Office, 1975), p. 78, n. 1.

6. See U.S., Congress, House, *Maximum Desirable Dimensions and Weights of Vehicles Operated on the Federal-Aid Systems,* 88th Cong., 2d sess., H. Doc. 354, 1964, p. 33.

7. Robley Winfrey et al., *Economics of the Maximum Limits of Motor Vehicle Dimensions and Weights,* 2 vols. (Washington, D.C.: Federal Highway Administration, Department of Transportation, 1974), 1:4–1.

8. See Malcolm F. Kent, "The Freight's the Weight," *Proceedings of the Thirty-Seventh Annual Meeting of the Highway Research Board, January 6–10, 1958* (Washington, D.C.: National Academy of Sciences, National Research Council, 1958), pp. 35–36.

9. American Trucking Associations, "The Case for Twin Trailers," 4th ed. (1974), p. 3, citing A. T. Kearney and Company, "An Economic Evaluation of Container Size Standards."

10. Ibid.

11. *American Trucking Trends 1974* (Washington, D.C.: American Trucking Associations, 1974), p. 34.

12. U.S., Department of Transportation, *Highway Statistics, 1973,* p. 261.

13. U.S., Congress, House, Committee on Public Works, Subcommittee on Roads, *Vehicle Weight and Dimension Limitations,* Hearing, 91st Cong., 1st sess., July 8–September 4, 1969, p. 69.

14. U.S., Congress, *Maximum Desirable Dimensions and Weights of Vehicles Operated on the Federal-Aid Systems,* p. 65.

15. Robert E. Whiteside et al., *Changes in Legal Vehicle Weights and Dimensions: Some Economic Effects on Highways,* National Cooperative Highway Research Program Report 141 (Washington, D.C.: Highway Research Board, National Research Council, National Academy of Sciences, National Academy of Engineering, 1973), p. 39

16. See U.S., Congress, Senate, Committee on Public Works, Subcommittee on Transportation, *Transportation and the New Energy Policies (Truck Sizes and Weights),* Part 2, Hearing, 93rd Cong., 2d sess., February 20–21 and March 26, 1974, p. 59.

17. U.S., Department of Transportation, Federal Highway Administration, "Effects of Increasing Truck Size and Weight on Increase in Freight Handling Capacity Per Truck Unit," mimeographed draft (1975), p. 4.

18. Ibid.

19. Whiteside et al., op. cit., p. 38.

20. Winfrey et al., op. cit., 1:4–6.

21. Ibid., 1:4–7, 4–9.

22. Ibid., 1:4–9, 4–10.

23. Ibid., 1:4–11.

24. U.S., Congress, *Maximum Desirable Dimensions and Weights of Vehicles Operated on the Federal-Aid Systems,* p. 94

25. Ibid.

26. Ibid., p. 98.

27. Ibid., p. 97.

28. Winfrey et al., op. cit., 1:4–12.

29. Ibid., 1:4–20.

30. FWHA Task Force on Size and Weight Limitations of Trucks, "Effects of Increasing Truck Size and Weight on Highway Design to Accommodate Different Off-Tracking Characteristics," Interim Report, (mimeographed) draft (February 21, 1975), p. 1, item 12.

31. Winfrey et al., op. cit., 1:4–31.

32. John J. O'Mara in U.S., Congress, *Vehicle Weight and Dimension Limitations,* p. 346.

33. Winfrey et al., op. cit., 1:4–32, 4–33.

34. U.S., Congress, *Maximum Desirable Dimensions and Weights of Vehicles Operated on the Federal-Aid Systems,* p. 1.

35. Winfrey et al., op. cit., 1:4–11.

36. FWHA Task Force, "Effects of Increasing Truck Size and Weight on Increase in Freight Handling Capacity Per Truck Unit," Table 3.

37. Winfrey et al., op. cit., 1:3–32.

38. U.S., Congress, *Transportation and the New Energy Policies (Truck Sizes and Weights)*, p. 439

39. Ibid.

40. Hoy Stevens, "Line-Haul Trucking Costs Upgraded, 1964," Highway Research Record, no. 127 (Washington, D.C.: Highway Research Board, 1966), p. 20.

41. U.S., Congress, *Transportation and the New Energy Policies (Truck Sizes and Weights)*, p. 33.

42. U.S., Congress, *Maximum Desirable Dimensions and Weights of Vehicles Operated on the Federal-Aid Systems*, p. 113

43. Roy Jorgensen et al., *Oversize-Overweight Permit Operation on State Highways*, National Cooperative Highway Research Program Report 80 (Washington, D.C.: National Academy of Sciences, National Academy of Engineering, 1969), pp. 1–2.

4

A MODEL TO ASCERTAIN THE
EFFECT OF SIZE AND WEIGHT MAXIMUMS
UPON MOTOR CARRIER PRODUCTIVITY

This chapter formulates a simulation model that will enable a firm engaged in intercity trucking or a government unit to ascertain the economic effect of restrictive covenants in weight and dimension standards upon motor-carrier productivity. Once procured, this measure of productivity could in turn be applied by the user to calculate the ultimate impact of size and weight restrictions upon either motor-carrier revenues and profits or governmental fiscal flows. However, prior to the construction and preparation of a flowchart for such a model, the underlying rationalization behind simulation and its appropriateness to this particular situation should be examined in detail.

A simulation in a comprehensive sense is merely the representation of reality or the abstraction of a system that has its counterpart in the real world.[1] This abstraction or model is employed to effectuate experiments designed to reveal certain characteristics of the model by implication of the idea, system, or situation modeled. Computer modeling constitutes a subset of simulation and essentially entails programming a computer to exhibit selected features similar to those of the real-world system or situation. The phrase "selected features" implies a simplification of the real-world system by encompassing in the model only those elements and interactions pertinent to the study at hand.[2] This, of course, reflects back to the original delimitations imposed in the first chapter of this investigation.

Simulation models provide a unique opportunity to observe the behavior of a complex interactive system in situations where it is either too costly or impossible or impractical to experiment with the actual system under analysis.[3] A simulation, then, permits a system to be studied without actually being disturbed. In the case of motor-vehicle weight and dimension limitations, neither the various factions, nor the individual state legislatures, could conceivably agree on a uniform set of sizes and weights for empirical purposes.

A simulation can also contribute regarding the testing of policies for the future,[4] particularly in evaluating possible strategies for public policy.[5] In this respect, future truck size and weight legislation has public policy ramifications for both the productivity of the trucking industry and state and federal government fiscal flows.

MODEL DEVELOPMENT

The previous chapter's enumeration of current size and weight standards in the United States provided the bulk of data necessary to initialize the model. However, one additional component was essential—the relevant characteristics of the vehicles that were utilized in the study. Table 4.1 represents an estimated distribution of truck combinations in 1975 in terms of visual classes, as reported by the Department of Transportation. Because of relative numbers and adequacy of available data regarding vehicle characteristics, eight types of trailer combinations, classified by axle arrangement, were considered in this

TABLE 4.1

Estimated Distribution of Truck Combinations in 1975 by Visual Class

Vehicle Description	Estimated Number in 1975
Combination vehicles with semitrailers	
Three-axle (2–S1)	184,070
Four-axle (2–S2)	365,810
Five-axle (3–S2)	309,890
Total	859,770
Combination vehicles with full trailers	
Three-axle (3–1)	32,620
Four-axle (2–2)	51,260
Five-axle (2–3, 3–2)	34,950
Six-axle (3–3 or more)	9,320
Total	128,150
Combination vehicles with semitrailer and full trailer	
Five-axle or more	177,080
Total	177,080
Total combination vehicles	1,165,000

Source: U.S., Department of Transportation, Federal Highway Administration, "Effects of Increasing Truck Size and Weight on Increase in Freight Handling Capacity Per Truck Unit," mimeographed draft (1975).

study. These eight combinations were: 2-S1, 2-S2, 3-S2, 2-S1-2, 3-S1-2, 3-S2-2, 3-S2-3, and 3-S2-4, and represented configurations incorporating five different tractor sizes as well as five separate trailer lengths.

The dimensional facets and cubic capacity of the trailers that comprise these combinations are shown in Table 4.2, while axle and tare weight data are presented in Table 4.3. Three assumptions pertinent to this data should be noted. First, each tractor was assumed to pull only a trailer of specified length. Second, all trailers were presupposed to be of the dry-van variety. Third, all combinations were assumed to maximize either payload or cubic capacity, depending upon the density of the commodity being transported.

In the first two cases, tractors are able to pull trailers of various lengths as well as a wide spectrum of cargo bodies, such as refrigerated vans, tank bodies, and platform or flatbed bodies. Including these items is merely a function of the complexity of the simulation model and, thus, such items were eliminated in the interest of simplicity. The supposition that cubic capacity can be totally occupied is perhaps overly generous but can be defended. No empirical evidence exists to substantiate any particular ullage factor and, therefore, the use of such a factor would in itself be an arbitrary assumption.

Vehicles that did not cube out were presumed to transport a front-axle load of 10,000 pounds. Thus the maximum possible gross weight of any vehicle in a particular state could be ascertained by adding 10,000 pounds to the product of the single-axle limitation and the number of single axles,* and the product of the tandem-axle restriction and the number of tandem axles. Therefore, the feasible payload of any combination is dependent upon the single- and tandem-axle statutes of a particular state and can be computed by subtracting the total tare weight of the combination (see Table 4.3) from either the maximum allowable gross weight or the maximum possible gross weight, contingent on the vehicle and situation. The maximum possible gross weights by type of combination for three common axle weight statutes are depicted in Table 4.4

Table 4.5 shows for the various vehicle classifications the effect on gross vehicle weight of a 1,000-pound modification in the single- or tandem-axle standard. Together these tables illustrate the intricate relationship present between axle weights and gross vehicle weight. Only if a vehicle has a maximum gross weight subjacent to a state's legal limit can a benefit be derived from an axle-weight increase alone. Employing the same logic, only those vehicles with maximum possible gross weights that exceed state statutes may profit from any augmentation solely in gross weight. For example, by referring to

---

*Excluding, of course, the front axle. Therefore, in all calculations the number of single axles must be reduced by one.

TABLE 4.2

Dimensions and Cubic Capacity of Trailers Utilized in Simulation Model (in feet)

Axle Classification	Width		Height		Length				Cubic Capacity
					First Trailer		Second Trailer		
	Outside	Inside	Outside	Inside	Outside	Inside	Outside	Inside	
2-S1	8.0	7.71	13.5	8.5	35.0	34.67	*	—	2272
2-S2	8.0	7.71	13.5	8.5	40.0	39.67	—	—	2600
3-S2	8.0	7.71	13.5	8.5	45.0	44.67	—	—	2927
2-S1-2	8.0	7.71	13.5	8.5	27.0	26.67	27.0	26.67	3496
3-S1-2	8.0	7.71	13.5	8.5	27.0	26.67	27.0	26.67	3496
3-S2-2	8.0	7.71	13.5	8.5	40.0	39.67	26.0	25.67	4282
3-S2-2	8.0	7.71	13.5	8.5	40.0	39.67	40.0	39.67	5200
3-S2-4	8.0	7.71	13.5	8.5	45.0	44.67	45.0	44.67	5854

*Dashes indicate category not applicable.

Note: Cubic capacity was calculated as the product of the inside dimensions for each trailer.

Source: Adapted from American Trucking Associations, "Typical Present Tractor, Dolly, and Trailer Weights and Dimensions," (mimeographed, n.d.)

TABLE 4.3

Characteristics of Tractor and Trailer Combinations Utilized in Simulation Model

Type of Combination, Axle Code Classification	Tractor Semitrailer			Tractor Semitrailer and Full				
	2–S1	2–S2	3–S2	2–S1–2	3–S1–2	3–S2–2	3–S2–3	3–S2–4
Number of axles on power unit	2	2	3	2	3	3	3	3
Number of axles on first trailer	1	2	2	1	1	2	2	2
Number of axles on second trailer	—*	—	—	2	2	2	2	4
Tare weight of tractor in pounds	5,800	10,500	15,270	12,223	15,270	15,270	16,500	16,500
Tare weight of first trailer in pounds	6,800	11,000	11,750	7,000	7,000	11,000	11,000	11,750
Tare weight of second trailer in pounds	—	—	—	7,000	7,000	7,000	11,000	11,750
Tare weight of converter dolly in pounds	—	—	—	2,467	2,467	2,467	2,467	4,500
Total tare weight and combination in pounds	12,600	21,500	27,020	28,690	31,737	35,737	41,967	44,500

*Dashes indicate category not applicable.

Sources: American Trucking Associations, "Typical Present Tractor, Dolly, and Trailer Weights and Dimensions," mimeogrpahed, n.d.; Hoy Stevens, Line-Haul Trucking Costs in Relation to Vehicle Gross Weights, Highway Research Board, Bulletin 301 (Washington, D.C.: National Academy of Sciences, National Research Council, 1961), p. 69.

TABLE 4.4

Maximum Possible Gross Weight by Type of Trailer Combination for Three Common Axle Weight Limitations

	Single Axle/Tandem Axle Gross Weight		
Vehicle Classification	18,000/32,000 Pounds	20,000/34,000 Pounds	22,000/36,000 Pounds
2–S1	46,000	50,000	54,800
2–S2	60,000	64,000	68,400
3–S3	74,000	78,000	82,000
2–S1–2	82,000	90,000	99,600
3–S1–2	96,000	104,000	113,200
3–S2–2	110,000	118,000	126,800
3–S2–3	124,000	132,000	140,400
3–S2–4	138,000	146,000	154,000

Note: Assumes a front-axle load of 10,000 pounds.
Source: Compiled by the authors.

TABLE 4.5

Effect of 1,000 Pound Alteration of Axle Weights on Possible Gross Vehicle Weight by Type of Combination

Vehicle Classification	Number of Axles		Alteration, in Pounds		Possible Increase in Gross Vehicle Weight, in Pounds
	Single	Tandem	Single Axle	Tandem Axle	
2–S1	3	0	1,000		2,000
				—*	—
2–S2	2	1	1,000		1,000
				1,000	1,000
3–S2	1	2	—		—
				1,000	2,000
2–S1–2	5	0	1,000		4,000
				—	—
3–S1–2	4	1	1,000		3,000
				1,000	1,000
3–S2–2	3	2	1,000		2,000
				1,000	2,000
3–S2–3	2	3	1,000		1,000
				1,000	3,000
3–S2–4	1	4	—		—
				1,000	4,000

*Dashes indicate category not applicable.
Source: Compiled by the authors.

Table 4.5, the 2-S1 vehicle category obviously could gain 2,000 pounds in payload from a 1,000-pound addition to any state's single-axle limitation. By recalling from Chapter 3 that the minimum gross weight restriction is 73,000 pounds and, moreover, by consulting Table 4.4, this advantage could apparently be fully accomodated in any state. Conversely, with present state standards, expanding gross vehicle weight to 90,000 pounds would serve no useful purpose for the 2-S1 vehicles without a sizable accompanying single-axle weight increase.

Additional Relationships And Delimitations

In the model, productivity loss is calculated on the basis of a fully loaded vehicle traveling in a single direction. Once again, as representation of the entire actual system was not a condition for accuracy, return load considerations were ignored. Productivity gain or loss was confined to that which was directly attributable to restrictive covenants in sizes and weights among the states, that is, either a change in cubic capacity, permissible payload, or both. The procedure for calculating the payload of a vehicle was elaborated upon earlier. This figure divided by the cubic capacity of the combination produced an optimum commodity density for the vehicle. Transportation of a commodity of this particular density will cause simultaneous optimization of both the size and weight restrictions. Hauling a commodity whose density exceeds the optimal density may be interpreted as weighting out; contrarily, a density that is lower than the optimum will cause the vehicle to cube out. Table 4.6 details the relationship and influence upon cubic capacity of a modification in any of the three dimensional factors. Width and height both generate proportional increases or decreases in total cubic capacity contingent upon the length of the vehicle, whereas a length alteration always modifies cubic capacity by a specific number of cubic feet, depending, of course, upon vehicle width and height.

TABLE 4.6

Dimensional Factors and Their Effect on Cubic Capacity

Dimensional Factor	Effect of Altering Dimensional Factor on Total Cubic Capacity	Total Gain or Loss in Cubic Capacity for Each Six Inches of Difference, in Cubic Feet
Width	proportional deviation	4.250 X length
Height	proportional deviation	3.855 X length
Length	fixed deviation	32.7675

Source: Compiled by the authors.

A vehicle's cubic capacity, which is indirectly linked to a state's size limitations, together with the weight statutes of a particular state, serve to ascertain the optimally dense commodity that can be transported by a vehicle within the confines of that state. But the problem of assessing optimal density is further compounded by the two classifications of highways within each state, that is, interstate and noninterstate. (Excepting Alaska, which has no interstate network.) Weight and dimension restrictions are frequently disparate on both categories of intrastate roads. Table 4.7 exhibits the extent to which this discrepancy presently exists. Twenty-five states have at least one factor whose limitation is determined by the highway system being traversed. An additional factor that certainly merits attention is that several states maintain a higher gross weight limitation which applies to designated highways only. This means that vehicles operated in certain states confront three possible distinct gross weights.* In view of this situation, an assumption was made that in any state a vehicle was constrained by the restrictions imposed on the highway system over which it traveled. Vehicles that moved over both interstate and noninterstate systems were governed by the sizes and weights of the stringent system unless transit over designated roads was stipulated. In the latter case, a truck on designated roads could operate utilizing the state's maximum gross weight

TABLE 4.7

Summary of Intrastate Dissimilarities on Interstate and Noninterstate Highways

Factor(s)	Number of States
Width only	1
Width and tandem axle	2
Width and gross weight*	2
Width, tandem, and gross weight*	1
Single and tandem axle	2
Tandem axle only	4
Tandem and gross weight*	4
Gross weight only*	7
Single, tandem, and gross weight*	2
Total	25

*Gross weight category includes allowances on designated highways.
Source: Compiled by the authors.

---

*Actually, only two states, Kansas and Nevada, have three different weights. However, there are seven other states whose designated highway gross weight exceeds gross weight allowance on noninterstate roads.

allowance. Hence, through input, a user of the model could control the high-way system under which his vehicle would be regulated.

Since both firms and government units were designated as potential adopters of the model, a certain degree of additional flexibility could be constructed into the model. From the managerial perspective of a given business, three potential questions dealing with productivity loss were presumed to exist with which the model should possess the capability to deal. First, what diminishment is associated with intrastate travel commensurable to maximum U. S. weights and dimensions? Second, what is the multistate trip loss incurred within a specific motor-carrier route configuration? Last, in a similar multi-state trip, what reduction occurs as compared to maximum U. S. standards?

On the other hand, a government unit's concern rests almost exclusively with productivity and its relationship to the flow of tax revenue, or the effect a proposed weight and length alteration will have upon these revenues.* In this regard, the model was constructed to accommodate inquiries by either an individual state government or the federal government relative to the productivity consequences of a modification in any one of 13 size and weight categories.† But, examination of more than one factor at a time was not allowed in the model.

Two final points could be delineated with respect to this analysis. The first concerns oversize-overweight permit operation, a topic previously discussed in Chapter 3. This operation was not included as an integral element in the construction of the model. Nevertheless, by adjusting state statutory limitations upward, the oversize-overweight facet can readily be incorporated into the model.

The second item to be delineated relates to the operation of twin trailers. Table 4.8 presents the cogent factors pertinent to this matter. Since 16 states prohibit the operation of twin trailers, a combination may conceivably be legally permitted to operate in one state of a specific route and yet not in another state. To calculate a productivity loss under these circumstances would be fallacious since the combination would simply be broken down into two shorter vehicles at the state line of the proscribing state.‡ In the case where

---

*For instance, a state trucking official has recently stated that for a 9.17 percent increase in allowable gross weight, truckers in that state are willing to pay 19.55 percent in additional gross-weight fees.

†These are interstate width, noninterstate width, height, truck-tractor semitrailer length, other combination length, designated highway length, interstate single-axle weight, noninterstate single-axle weight, interstate tandem-axle weight, noninterstate tandem-axle weight, interstate gross weight, noninterstate gross weight, and designated highway gross weight.

‡It is recognized that this constitutes a productivity loss in the sense that an additional driver and tractor are required. However, this exceeds the scope of the originally conceived definition of productivity in this study, that is, loss of cubic capacity and/or payload.

TABLE 4.8

Resolution of Twin Trailer Activity in the Model

Multistate Trip Conditions	Computer Output	Explanation
Combination is legally permitted in at least one state and not permitted in at least one state on the designated route.	NC	Vehicle can be broken down at the border. Hence, productivity loss is not computed.
Combination is prohibited in at least one state and the length limitation of at least one other state is exceeded.	NP	Vehicle is not permitted. Hence, productivity loss cannot be computed.
Combination is not permitted in any state on the designated route.	*	Productivity loss computed as an opportunity loss.

Source: Compiled by the authors.

the combination is interdicted in one state and has a physical length that is not sanctioned in another state, any productivity loss can again not be ascertained. (In this case there is no common frame of reference upon which to base an opportunity loss.) Yet, in the third case, where the vehicle is unauthorized to travel for the same reason in all states under consideration, productivity losses can be ascertained on all opportunity-loss bases. That is, the calculation of the opportunity loss depends upon which size and weight factors are involved.

Formulation of the Model

The initialization process entails introducing into the simulation model both the size and weight data detailed in depth in Chapter 3 and the truck data adumbrated in an earlier section of this chapter. Once this step is accomplished, two major branches in the model are allowed. The selection of the appropriate segment hinges upon an input variable that denotes whether the user is a firm or a government unit.

If examination of this input variable reveals that the user is a firm, four additional variables are required as model inputs. These include: the vehicle combination type under consideration; the density of the commodity being transported; the individual state information disclosing the percentage of ton-miles operated on interstate and noninterstate highways; and whether or not travel on designated highways will occur and the type of simulation to be conducted. The significance of this information is that the vehicle combination type manifests maximum cubic capacity and supplies the data necessary to compute maximum allowable gross weight, given a particular state. The reader will recall that these two items are essential in the calculation of the optimum commodity density which can be hauled by a specific vehicle; the relationship between the density of the commodity being transported and the vehicle's optimum density decides whether weight or dimensional elements are involved; state highway input data stipulates which system will govern the relevant factors; and the type of simulation defaults to a comparison with maximum U. S. standards if only one state is involved. Otherwise, the user must designate whether productivity loss is to be computed solely on the basis of the largest limitations within the route configuration or on the basis of maximum U.S. weights or some other dimensions.

Once these preliminary details are lucidly defined, the subsequent step necessitates calculations of maximum allowable payload and optimum commodity density. The differential between maximum payload and maximum allowable payload is that the former excludes the gross-weight limitation from consideration. Maximum allowable payload is maximum payload as long as the gross-weight restriction is not exceeded. If maximum payload is greater than allowable gross weight, gross weight becomes the maximum allowable payload and the procedure for calculating payload and optimum density has been described in an earlier section. Comparison of the values for commodity and optimal density establishes a three-way conditional branch that may be regarded as cubing out if commodity density is below optimum density, and weighing out if commodity density is larger than optimum density, and "simultaneous optimization" if commodity and optimum density are equal.

In the first case, only dimensional factors are relevant, as additional weight allowance fails to benefit a vehicle whose interior capacity is filled. Once the proper path has been selected, there remains the process of determining which type of simulation has been designated. In any event, percentage productivity loss ascribable to dimensional factors will always consist of comparing individual size categories against some maximum standard. For single-state comparisons, the dimensions permitted in the designated state are measured against maximum U. S. standards. For more than one state, the comparison will always consist of the smallest sizes within the route against either the largest in the route or the U. S. maximum standards.

In the event that the second branch has been followed, the weight factors become crucial and size factors can be ignored. Since a maximum allowable payload in the state of origin is already stored and if a single-state comparison has been designated, another payload is calculated using the appropriate U.S. maximum single-axle, tandem-axle, and gross-weight limitations. The principle of payload and allowable payload likewise extends to this particular computation. Productivity loss as a percentage is expressed by subtracting the state payload from the U. S. maximum payload and dividing by the state payload. For multistate-route losses, two payloads are still needed. However, the payloads under consideration are based on either the smallest and largest weights on the route or the smallest weights on the route versus U. S. maximum restrictions. These correspond to designations of multistate-route productivity loss and multistate loss compared to U. S. maximum weights, respectively.

In the event of simultaneous optimization, the problem is that the vehicle is weighing out and cubing out concurrently. This requires the setting of a variable such that both previous paths may be freely accessed and departed in order that the productivity loss from both the size and weight factors be summed.

If the user of the model represents a government unit, there are four variables that must be clearly defined. These are: the type of government unit, the vehicle combination type under consideration, the category of size or weight change under consideration, and the actual change itself. The primary purpose of this information is fourfold: the type of government unit determines whether a single state or all states are to be included in the simulation; vehicle combination type serves the same function as in the firm segment; the category of size or weight change simply specifies what is to be altered and on which highway system;* and the actual change is the new numeric limitation, in either inches, feet, or pounds, of the weight or dimension classification.

From a procedural perspective, there is minute, if any, difference in the functioning of the two segments of the model subsequent to this position. If a state government has been designated, two comparisons are still required but there is no longer strictly the concept of productivity loss. Instead of the large-small relationship that predominates the firm segment, the government-unit portion of the model ascertains productivity change on a before-after basis within a single state. Thus, a contemplated change may produce a productivity loss or gain depending upon its relationship to current standards. This principle is extended to encompass all states if the federal government is the user. In order that both of the previously presented segments may be totally envisaged, a system flowchart for the entire size and weight model is presented in Figure 4.1.

DESCRIPTION AND ANALYSIS OF TESTING THE MODEL

The Testing Procedure

The model's greatest asset, generality, proved to be a formidable problem in the determination of an appropriate application for the model. Obviously, in the firm segment, it was neither practical nor conceivable to simulate every

---

*See † note on page 83.

FIGURE 4.1

System Flowchart of the Size and Weight Model

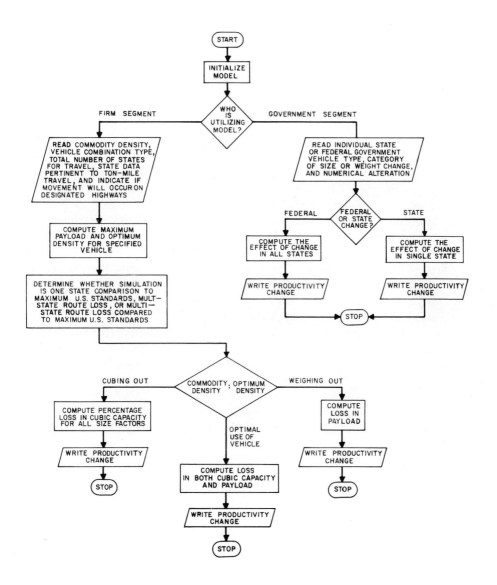

Source: Compiled by the authors.

possible route configuration for all combinations of vehicles, on all highway systems in the United States. Likewise, in the government segment no method existed to account for all changes, in all categories, for all vehicles, on all domestic highway systems. The question arose, therefore, as to how these countless combinations could be effectively delimited.

In the firm portion of the model, both the interstate and noninterstate systems were represented, as were all vehicle combinations included in the study. Additionally, a simulated operation of the various combinations constrained first by size factors and second by weight limitations was deemed necessary. In this regard, Table 4.9 focuses on the question of pertinent routes. Between 1960 and 1973, the average length of a freight haul by class I common carrier remained relatively stable at between 256 and 280 statute miles. Assuming that the class I figure is a route indicator of the industry average, this suggests that any nonspecific analyses would best be confined to a small number of contiguous states. Therefore, all 108 two-state route combinations incorporating all of the previously selected elements were selected for simulation in the firm segment. The results of this endeavor are exhibited in Tables 4.10, 4.11, 4.12, and 4.13. Tables 4.10 and 4.11 illustrate the percentage productivity loss due to restrictive covenants in size maximums for the interstate and noninterstate highway systems respectively. Tables 4.12 and 4.13 disclose identical data for weight maximums.

In the government portion of the model, some recent size and weight recommendations were explored. The Winfrey Study's single- and tandem-axle weight limits were simulated over noninterstate highways for the 2-S2 vehicle

TABLE 4.9

Average Length of Freight Haul by Class I Common Carrier in Domestic Commerce (in statute miles)

Year	Length of Haul
1960	272
1965	259
1966	263
1967	256
1968	258
1969	261
1970	263
1971	277
1972	280
1973*	278

*Preliminary estimate.

Source: Transportation Association of America, *Transportation Facts and Trends* (Washington, D.C.: Transportation Association of America, December 1974), p. 14.

TABLE 4.10

Percentage Productivity Loss Due to Restrictive Covenants in Size Maximums of the
Interstate Highway System for All Two-State Route Combinations

Two-State Route	Percentage Productivity Loss by Vehicle Axle Code Classification							
	2–S1	2–S2	3–S2	2–S1–2	3–S1–2	3–S2–2	3–S2–3	3–S2–4
Alabama–Florida	0	0	0	19.440*	19.440*	46.293*	77.656*	100*
Alabama–Georgia	0	0	0	NP	NP	NP	NP	NP
Alabama–Mississippi	0	0	0	NP	NP	NP	NP	NP
Alabama–Tennessee	0	0	0	19.440*	19.440*	46.293*	77.656*	100*
Arizona–California	0	0	0	0	0	22.438*	48.741*	67.449*
Arizona–Colorado	0	0	0	0	0	22.483*	48.741*	67.449*
Arizona–Nevada	5.882	5.882	28.272	24.628	24.628	NC	NC	NC
Arizona–New Mexico	0	0	0	0	0	22.483*	48.741*	67.449*
Arizona–Utah	5.882	5.882	5.882	5.882	5.882	NC	NC	NC
Arkansas–Louisiana	0	0	11.195	0	0	22.483*	48.741*	67.449*
Arkansas–Mississippi	0	0	0	NC	NC	22.483*	48.741*	67.449*
Arkansas–Missouri	0	0	0	0	0	22.483*	48.741*	67.449*
Arkansas–Oklahoma	0	0	22.390	0	0	22.483*	48.741*	67.449*
Arkansas–Tennessee	0	0	0	NC	NC	NP	NP	NP
Arkansas–Texas	0	0	22.390	0	0	22.483*	48.741*	67.449*
California–Nevada	5.882	5.882	28.272	24.628	24.628	NC	NC	NC
California–Oregon	0	0	11.195	18.746	18.746	NC	NC	NC
Colorado–Kansas	0	0	11.195	0	0	NC	NC	NC
Colorado–Nebraska	0	0	11.195	0	0	22.483*	48.741*	67.449*
Colorado–New Mexico	0	0	0	0	0	22.483*	48.741*	67.449*
Colorado–Oklahoma	0	0	0	0	0	22.483*	48.741*	67.449*
Colorado–Utah	5.882	5.882	5.882	5.882	5.882	NC	NC	NC
Colorado–Wyoming	5.882	5.882	28.272	24.628	24.628	NC	21.439*	36.712*

(continued)

(Table 4.10 continued)

Percentage Productivity Loss by Vehicle Axle Code Classification

Two-State Route	2-S1	2-S2	3-S2	2-S1-2	3-S1-2	3-S2-2	3-S2-3	3-S2-4
Connecticut–Massachusetts	6.485	6.485	6.485	19.440*	19.440*	46.293*	77.656*	100*
Connecticut–New York	6.485	6.485	6.485	NC	NC	NC	NC	NC
Connecticut–Rhode Island	0	0	0	19.440*	19.440*	46.293*	77.656*	100*
Delaware–Maryland	0	0	0	0	0	22.483*	48.741*	67.449*
Delaware–New Jersey	0	0	0	NC	NC	22.483*	48.741*	67.449*
Delaware–Pennsylvania	0	0	0	NP	NP	NP	NP	NP
Florida–Georgia	0	0	0	NP	NP	NP	NP	NP
Georgia–North Carolina	0	0	0	NP	NP	NP	NP	NP
Georgia–South Carolina	0	0	0	NP	NP	NP	NP	NP
Georgia–Tennessee	0	0	0	NP	NP	NP	NP	NP
Idaho–Montana	5.882	5.882	17.007	34.001	34.001	25.778	NC	12.577*
Idaho–Nevada	0	5.882	22.390	0	0	10.713	8.822	NC
Idaho–Oregon	5.882	5.882	17.077	5.882	5.882	16.595	14.704	NC
Idaho–Utah	0	0	0	18.746	18.746	15.305	12.603	NC
Idaho–Washington	5.882	5.882	5.882	24.628	24.628	NC	NC	12.577*
Idaho–Wyoming	0	0	22.390	0	0	35.201	NC	NC
Illinois–Indiana	0	0	0	9.373	9.373	NC	NC	12.577*
Illinois–Iowa	0	0	0	NC	NC	22.483*	48.741*	67.449*
Illinois–Kentucky	0	0	0	9.373	9.373	22.483*	48.741*	67.449*
Illionis–Missouri	0	0	0	9.373	9.373	22.483*	48.741*	67.499*
Illinois–Wisconsin	0	0	0	NC	NC	NP	NP	NP
Indiana–Kentucky	0	0	0	0	0	NP	NP	NP
Indiana–Michigan	0	0	0	0	0	NC	NC	12.577*
Indiana–Ohio	0	0	0	0	0	0	0	12.577*
Iowa–Minnesota	0	0	0	NC	NC	22.483*	48.741*	67.449*
Iowa–Missouri	0	0	0	NC	NC	22.483*	48.741*	67.449*
Iowa–Nebraska	0	0	11.195	NC	NC	22.483*	48.741*	67.449*
Iowa–South Dakota	0	0	11.195	NC	NC	NP	21.439*	36.712*
Iowa–Wisconsin	0	0	0	NP	NP	NP	NP	NP
Kansas–Missouri	0	0	11.195	0	0	NC	NC	NC

Kansas–Nebraska	0	0	0	0	NC	NC	NC
Kansas–Oklahoma	0	0	11.195	0	NC	NC	NC
Kentucky–Missouri	0	0	0	0	22.483*	48.741*	67.449*
Kentucky–Ohio	0	0	0	NC	NC	NC	12.577*
Kentucky–Tennessee	0	0	0	NC	NP	NP	NP
Kentucky–Virginia	11.764	11.764	0	NC	NP	NP	NP
Kentucky–West Virginia	0	0	22.959	18.746	22.483*	48.741*	67.449*
Louisiana–Mississippi	0	0	11.195	18.746	22.483*	48.741*	67.449*
Louisiana–Texas	0	0	11.195	0	22.483*	48.741*	67.449*
Maine–New Hampshire	0	0	3.358	19.440*	46.293*	77.656*	100*
Maryland–Pennsylvania	0	0	0	NC	NP	NP	NP
Maryland–Virginia	11.764	11.764	0	NC	NP	NP	NP
Maryland–West Virginia	11.764	11.764	22.959	NC	NP	NP	NP
Maryland–District of Columbia	0	0	11.764	19.440*	46.293*	77.656*	NP
Massachusetts–New Hampshire	0	0	0	NC	NC	NC	100*
Massachusetts–New York	6.485	6.485	0	19.440*	46.293*	77.656*	NC
Massachusetts–Rhode Island	0	6.485	6.485	19.440*	46.293*	77.656*	100*
Massachusetts–Vermont	0	0	0	0	46.293*	77.656*	100*
Michigan–Ohio	0	0	0	18.746	NC	NC	12.577*
Minnesota–North Dakota	0	0	18.746	9.373	22.483*	48.741*	67.449*
Minnesota–South Dakota	0	0	9.373	NC	NC	21.439*	36.712*
Minnesota–Wisconsin	0	0	NC	NP	NP	NP	NP
Mississippi–Tennessee	0	0	NP	0	NP	NP	NP
Missouri–Nebraska	0	0	0	0	22.483*	48.714*	67.449*
Missouri–Oklahoma	0	0	0	NC	22.483*	48.741*	67.449*
Missouri–Tennessee	0	0	0	9.373	NP	NP	NP
Montana–North Dakota	0	0	11.195	0	NC	21.439*	36.712*
Montana–South Dakota	5.882	5.882	0	0	7.652	21.439*	36.712*
Montana–Wyoming	0	0	39.467	34.001	21.187	21.439*	36.712*
Nebraska–South Dakota	5.882	5.882	0	9.373	NC	21.439*	36.712*
Nebraska–Wyoming	5.882	5.882	39.467	24.628	NC	21.439*	36.712*

(continued)

(Table 4.10 continued)

Percentage Productivity Loss by Vehicle Axle Code Classification

Two-State Route	2–S1	2–S2	3–S2	2–S1–2	3–S1–2	3–S2–2	3–S2–3	3–S2–4
Nevada–Oregon	5.882	5.882	39.467	5.882	5.882	5.882	5.882	5.882
Nevada–Utah	0	0	22.390	18.747	18.746	4.591	3.781	3.358
New Hampshire–Vermont	0	0	0	19.440*	19.440*	46.293*	77.656*	100*
New Jersey–New York	0	0	0	NC	NC	NC	NC	NC
New Jersey–Pennsylvania	0	0	0	NP	NP	NP	NP	NP
New Mexico–Oklahoma	0	0	0	0	0	22.483*	48.741*	67.449*
New Mexico–Texas	0	0	0	0	0	22.483*	48.741*	67.449*
New Mexico–Utah	5.882	5.882	5.882	5.882	5.882	NC	NC	NC
New York–Pennsylvania	0	0	0	NC	NC	NC	NC	NC
New York–Vermont	0	0	0	NC	NC	NC	NC	NC
North Carolina–South Carolina	0	0	0	19.440*	19.440*	46.293*	77.656*	100*
North Carolina–Tennessee	0	0	0	19.440*	19.440*	46.293*	77.656*	100*
North Carolina–Virginia	0	0	0	19.440*	19.440*	46.293*	77.656*	100*
North Dakota–South Dakota	0	0	11.195	9.373	9.373	NC	21.439*	36.712*
Ohio–Pennsylvania	0	0	0	NC	NC	NC	NC	NP
Ohio–West Virginia	11.764	11.764	22.959	NC	NC	NC	NC	NP
Oklahoma–Texas	0	0	0	0	0	22.483*	48.741*	67.449*
Oregon–Washington	0	0	11.195	18.746	18.746	NC	NC	NC
Pennsylvania–West Virginia	11.764	11.764	22.959	19.440*	19.440*	46.293*	77.656*	100*
South Dakota–Wyoming	5.882	5.882	39.467	34.001	34.001	13.534	21.439*	36.712
Tennessee–Virginia	0	0	0	19.440*	19.440*	46.293	77.656*	100*
Utah–Wyoming	0	0	22.390	18.746	18.746	50.506	NC	NC
Virginia–West Virginia	11.764	11.764	22.959	19.440*	19.440*	46.293*	77.656*	100*
Virginia–District of Columbia	11.764	11.764	11.764	19.440*	19.440*	46.293*	77.656*	100*

*Combination not permitted in either state. Percentage loss based on difference in cubic capacity between this vehicle and maximum allowable vehicle in the state.

Note: NC = not calculated because combination is permitted in one state but not the other state; NP = combination is prohibited in one state and length limitation is exceeded in the other state.

Source: Compiled by the authors.

TABLE 4.11

Percentage Productivity Loss Due to Restrictive Covenants in Size Maximums of the Noninterstate Highway System for All Two-State Route Combinations

Two-State Route	Percentage Productivity Loss by Vehicle Axle Code Classification							
	2–S1	2–S2	3–S2	2–S1–2	3–S1–2	3–S2–2	3–S2–3	3–S2–4
Alabama–Florida	0	0	0	19.440*	19.440*	46.293*	77.656*	100*
Alabama–Georgia	0	0	0	NP	NP	NP	NP	NP
Alabama–Mississippi	0	0	0	NP	NP	NP	NP	NP
Alabama–Tennessee	0	0	0	19.440*	19.440*	46.293*	77.656*	100*
Arizona–California	0	0	0	0	0	22.483*	48.741*	67.449*
Arizona–Colorado	0	0	0	0	0	22.483*	48.741*	67.449*
Arizona–Nevada	5.882	5.882	28.272	24.628	24.628	NC	NC	NC
Arizona–New Mexico	0	0	0	0	0	22.483*	48.741*	67.449*
Arizona–Utah	5.882	5.882	5.882	5.882	5.882	NC	NC	NC
Arkansas–Louisiana	0	0	11.195	0	0	22.483*	48.741*	67.449*
Arkansas–Mississippi	0	0	0	NC	NC	22.483*	48.741*	67.449*
Arkansas–Missouri	0	0	0	0	0	22.483*	48.741*	67.449*
Arkansas–Oklahoma	0	0	22.390	0	0	22.483*	48.741*	67.449*
Arkansas–Tennessee	0	0	0	NC	NC	NP	NP	NP
Arkansas–Texas	0	0	22.390	0	0	22.483*	48.741*	67.449*
California–Nevada	5.882	5.882	28.272	24.628	24.628	NC	NC	NC
California–Oregon	0	0	11.195	18.746	18.746	NC	NC	NC
Colorado–Kansas	0	0	11.195	0	0	NC	NC	NC
Colorado–Nebraska	0	0	11.195	0	0	22.483*	48.741*	67.449*
Colorado–New Mexico	0	0	0	0	0	22.483*	48.741*	67.449*
Colorado–Oklahoma	0	0	0	0	0	22.483*	48.741*	67.449*
Colorado–Utah	5.882	5.882	5.882	5.882	5.882	NC	NC	NC
Colorado–Wyoming	12.367	12.367	34.757	31.113	31.113	NC	21.439*	36.712*

(continued)

(Table 4.11 continued)

Percentage Productivity Loss by Vehicle Axle Code Classification

Two-State Route	2-S1	2-S2	3-S2	2-S1-2	3-S1-2	3-S2-2	3-S2-3	3-S2-4
Connecticut–Massachusetts	6.485	6.485	6.485	19.440*	19.440*	46.293*	77.656*	100*
Connecticut–New York	6.485	6.485	6.485	NC	NC	NC	NC	NC
Connecticut–Rhode Island	0	0	0	19.440*	19.440*	46.293*	77.656*	100*
Delaware–Maryland	0	0	0	0	0	22.483*	48.741*	67.449*
Delaware–New Jersey	0	0	0	NC	NC	22.483*	48.741*	67.449*
Delaware–Pennsylvania	0	0	0	NC	NC	NP	NP	NP
Florida–Georgia	0	0	0	NP	NP	NP	NP	NP
Georgia–North Carolina	0	0	0	NP	NP	NP	NP	NP
Georgia–South Carolina	0	0	0	NP	NP	NP	NP	NP
Georgia–Tennessee	0	0	0	NP	NP	NP	NP	NP
Idaho–Montana	5.882	5.882	17.077	34.001	34.001	25.778	NC	12.577*
Idaho–Nevada	6.485	6.485	28.875	6.485	6.485	17.198	15.307	NC
Idaho–Oregon	12.367	12.367	23.562	12.367	12.367	23.080	21.189	NC
Idaho–Utah	6.485	6.485	6.485	25.231	25.231	21.790	19.088	NC
Idaho–Washington	12.367	12.367	12.367	31.113	31.113	NC	NC	12.577 *
Idaho–Wyoming	0	0	22.390	0	0	35.201	NC	NC
Illinois–Indiana	0	0	0	9.373	9.373	NC	NC	12.577*
Illinois–Iowa	0	0	0	NC	NC	22.483*	48.741*	67.449*
Illinois–Kentucky	0	0	0	9.373	9.373	22.483*	48.741*	67.449*
Illionis–Missouri	0	0	0	9.373	9.373	22.483*	48.741*	67.499*
Illinois–Wisconsin	0	0	0	NC	NC	NP	NP	NP
Indiana–Kentucky	0	0	0	0	0	NC	NC	12.577*
Indiana–Michigan	0	0	0	0	0	NC	NC	12.577*
Indiana–Ohio	0	0	0	0	0	0	0	12.577*
Iowa–Minnesota	0	0	0	NC	NC	22.483*	48.741*	67.449*
Iowa–Missouri	0	0	0	NC	NC	22.483*	48.741*	67.449*
Iowa–Nebraska	0	0	11.195	NC	NC	22.483*	48.741*	67.449*
Iowa–South Dakota	0	0	11.195	NC	NC	NC	21.439*	36.712*
Iowa–Wisconsin	0	0	0	NP	NP	NP	NP	NP

94

Kansas–Missouri	0	0	11.195	0	NC	NC	NC
Kansas–Nebraska	0	0	0	0	NC	NC	NC
Kansas–Oklahoma	0	0	11.195	0	NC	NC	NC
Kentucky–Missouri	0	0	0	0	22.483*	48.741*	67.449*
Kentucky–Ohio	0	0	0	NC	NP	NC	12.577*
Kentucky–Tennessee	0	0	0	NC	NP	NP	NP
Kentucky–Virginia	11.764	11.764	22.959	NC	NP	NP	NP
Kentucky–West Virginia	0	0	11.195	NC	NP	NP	NP
Louisiana–Mississippi	0	0	11.195	0	22.483*	48.741*	67.449*
Louisiana–Texas	6.485	6.485	9.843	0	22.483*	48.741*	67.449*
Maine–New Hampshire	0	0	0	19.440*	46.293*	77.656*	100*
Maryland–Pennsylvania	11.764	11.764	0	NC	NP	NP	NP
Maryland–Virginia	11.764	11.764	22.959	NC	NP	NP	NP
Maryland–West Virginia	0	0	11.764	NC	NP	NP	NP
Maryland–District of Columbia	6.485	6.485	0	NC	NP	NP	NP
Massachusetts–New Hampshire	0	0	0	19.440*	46.293*	77.656*	100*
Massachusetts–New York	0	0	6.485	NC	NC	NC	NC
Massachusetts–Rhode Island	0	0	0	19.440*	46.293*	77.656*	100*
Massachusetts–Vermont	6.485	6.485	0	19.440*	46.293*	77.656*	100*
Michigan–Ohio	0	0	28.875	0	NC	NC	12.577*
Minnesota–North Dakota	0	0	11.195	25.231	22.483*	48.741*	67.449*
Minnesota–South Dakota	0	0	0	9.373	NC	21.439	36.712*
Minnesota–Wisconsin	0	0	0	NC	NP	NP	NP
Mississippi–Tennessee	0	0	11.195	NP	NP	NP	NP
Missouri–Nebraska	0	0	22.390	0	22.483*	48.741*	67.449*
Missouri–Oklahoma	0	0	0	0	22.483*	48.741*	67.449*
Missouri–Tennessee	0	0	11.195	NC	NC	NP	NP
Montana–North Dakota	6.485	6.485	6.485	9.373	14.137	21.439*	36.712*
Montana–South Dakota	5.882	6.485	0	6.485	21.187	21.439*	36.712*
Montana–Wyoming	5.882	5.882	39.467	34.001	NC	21.439*	36.712*
Nebraska–South Dakota	0	0	0	9.373	NC	21.439*	36.712*
Nebraska–Wyoming	12.367	12.367	45.952	31.113	NC	21.439*	36.712*

(continued)

(Table 4.11 continued)

Percentage Productivity Loss by Vehicle Axle Code Classification

Two-State Route	2–S1	2–S2	3–S2	2–S1–2	3–S1–2	3–S2–2	3–S2–3	3–S2–4
Nevada–Oregon	5.882	5.882	39.467	5.882	5.882	5.882	5.882	5.882
Nevada–Utah	0	0	22.390	18.747	18.746	4.591	3.781	3.358
New Hampshire–Vermont	0	0	0	19.440*	19.440*	46.293*	77.656*	100*
New Jersey–New York	0	0	0	NC	NC	NC	NC	NC
New Jersey–Pennsylvania	0	0	0	NP	NP	NP	NP	NP
New Mexico–Oklahoma	0	0	0	0	0	22.483*	48.741*	67.449*
New Mexico–Texas	0	0	0	0	0	22.483*	48.741*	67.449*
New Mexico–Utah	5.882	5.882	5.882	5.882	5.882	NC	NC	NC
New York–Pennsylvania	0	0	0	NC	NC	NC	NC	NC
New York–Vermont	0	0	0	NC	NC	NC	NC	NC
North Carolina–South Carolina	0	0	0	19.440*	19.440*	46.293*	77.656*	100*
North Carolina–Tennessee	0	0	0	19.440*	19.440*	46.293*	77.656*	100*
North Carolina–Virginia	0	0	0	19.440*	19.440*	46.293*	77.656*	100*
North Dakota–South Dakota	6.485	6.485	17.680	15.858	15.858	NC	21.439*	36.712*
Ohio–Pennsylvania	11.764	0	0	NC	NC	NC	NC	NP
Ohio–West Virginia	11.764	11.764	22.959	NC	NC	NC	NC	NP
Oklahoma–Texas	0	0	0	0	0	22.483*	48.741*	67.449*
Oregon–Washington	0	0	11.195	18.746	18.746	NC	NC	NC
Pennsylvania–West Virginia	11.764	11.764	22.959	19.440*	19.440*	46.293*	77.656*	100*
South Dakota–Wyoming	12.367	12.367	45.952	40.486	40.486	20.019	21.439*	36.712*
Tennessee–Virginia	0	0	0	19.440*	19.440*	46.293*	77.656*	100*
Utah–Wyoming	6.485	6.485	28.875	25.231	25.231	56.991	NC	NC
Virginia–West Virginia	11.764	11.764	22.959	19.440*	19.440*	46.293*	77.656*	100*
Virginia–District of Columbia	11.764	11.764	11.764	19.440*	19.440*	46.293*	77.656*	100*

*Combination is permitted in either state. Percentage loss based on difference in cubic capacity between this vehicle and maximum allowable vehicle in the state.

Note: NC = not calculated because combination is permitted in one state but not the other state; NP = combination is prohibited in one state and length limitation is exceeded in the other state.

Source: Compiled by the authors.

TABLE 4.12

Percentage Productivity Loss Due to Restrictive Covenants in Weight Maximums on the Interstate Highway System for All Two-State Route Combinations

Two-State Route	Percentage Productivity Loss by Vehicle Axle Code Classification							
	2–S1	2–S2	3–S2	2–S1–2	3–S1–2	3–S2–2	3–S2–3	3–S2–4
Alabama–Florida	10.695	13.306	0	0*	0*	0*	0*	0*
Alabama–Georgia	1.82	2.952	0	NP	NP	NP	NP	NP
Alabama–Mississippi	11.976	24.935	14.527	NP	NP	NP	NP	NP
Alabama–Tennessee	11.976	24.935	14.527	0*	0*	0*	0*	0*
Arizona–California	0	0	0	0	0	0*	0*	0*
Arizona–Colorado	0	4.706	3.923	0	0	0*	0*	0*
Arizona–Nevada	0	0	0	0	0	NC	NC	NC
Arizona–New Mexico	8.556	4.518	1.255	12.473	13.261	14.459*	16.827*	18.028*
Arizona–Utah	0	4.706	7.846	15.377	16.348	NC	NC	NC
Arkansas–Louisiana	11.976	10.390	10.203	15.071	16.176	17.899*	21.461*	23.350*
Arkansas–Mississippi	0	0	0	NC	NC	0*	0*	0*
Arkansas–Missouri	0	0	0	0	0	0*	0*	0*
Arkansas–Oklahoma	11.976	10.390	10.203	15.071	16.176	17.899*	21.461*	23.350*
Arkansas–Tennessee	0	0	0	NC	NC	NP	NP	NP
Arkansas–Texas	11.976	10.390	10.203	15.071	16.176	17.899*	21.461*	23.350*
California–Nevada	0	0	0	0	0	NC	NC	NC
California–Oregon	0	0	0	19.489	49.728	NC	NC	NC
Colorado–Kansas	0	4.706	3.923	0	0	NC	NC	NC
Colorado–Nebraska	0	4.706	20.065	20.855	22.467	25.005*	30.344*	34.228*
Colorado–New Mexico	8.556	7.660	2.635	12.473	13.261	14.459*	16.827*	18.028*
Colorado–Oklahoma	0	4.706	3.923	0	0	0*	0*	0*
Colorado–Utah	0	0	3.775	15.377	16.348	NC	NC	NC
Colorado–Wyoming	0	0	0	0	0	NC	NC	NC

(continued)

(Table 4.12   continued)

Percentage Productivity Loss by Vehicle Axle Code Classification

Two-State Route	2-S1	2-S2	3-S2	2-S1-2	3-S1-2	3-S2-2	3-S2-3	3-S2-4
Connecticut–Massachusetts	2.123	2.490	15.224	15.798*	16.964*	18.785*	22.557*	24.561*
Connecticut–New York	2.123	2.490	15.224	NC	NC	NC	NC	NC
Connecticut–Rhode Island	2.123	2.490	25.325	33.640*	36.107*	39.954*	47.903*	52.120*
Delaware–Maryland	12.834	14.382	0	0	0	0*	0*	0*
Delaware–New Jersey	18.824	12.988	16.364	NC	NC	20.164*	24.175*	26.303*
Delaware–Pennsylvania	16.417	9.326	0	NC	NC	NP	NP	NP
Florida–Georgia	8.718	10.057	0	NP	NP	NP	NP	NP
Georgia–North Carolina	1.818	11.281	0.379	NP	NP	NP	NP	NP
Georgia–South Carolina	8.718	6.495	1.148	NP	NP	NP	NP	NP
Georgia–Tennessee	14.012	28.623	14.527	NP	NP	NP	NP	0*
Idaho–Montana	0	0	0	0	0	0	NC	NC
Idaho–Nevada	0	0	2.411	6.651	7.101	7.793	9.187	NC
Idaho–Oregon	0	0	2.411	27.437	60.360	69.893	82.393	NC
Idaho–Utah	0	4.706	10.446	23.051	24.610	27.007	31.838	NC
Idaho–Washington	0	0	1.633	1.691	1.807	NC	NC	2.540*
Idaho–Wyoming	0	4.706	6.428	6.651	7.101	7.793	NC	NC
Illinois–Indiana	0	0	0	0	0	NC	NC	0*
Illinois–Iowa	3.234	3.896	0	NC	NC	0*	0*	0*
Illinois–Kentucky	11.976	10.390	10.203	15.071	16.176	17.899*	21.461*	23.350*
Illionis–Missouri	0	0	0	0	0	0*	0*	0*
Illinois–Wisconsin	8.982	3.896	0.609	NC	NC	NP	NP	NP
Indiana–Kentucky	11.976	10.390	10.203	15.071	16.176	NC	NC	23.350*
Indiana–Michigan	0	0	1.556	19.556	54.690	NC	NC	217.929*
Indiana–Ohio	11.976	10.390	10.203	15.071	16.176	17.899	21.461	23.350*
Iowa–Minnesota	3.234	3.896	0	NC	NC	0*	0*	0*
Iowa–Missouri	3.234	3.896	0	NC	NC	0*	0*	0*
Iowa–Nebraska	8.469	6.250	4.836	NC	NC	6.027*	7.313*	8.009*
Iowa–South Dakota	8.469	6.250	10.203	NC	NC	NC	21.461*	23.350*
Iowa–Wisconsin	5.568	6.612	0.609	NP	NP	NP	NP	NP

Kansas–Missouri	11.976	10.390	10.203	15.071	16.176	NC	NC	NC
Kansas–Nebraska	0	0	15.533	20.855	22.467	NC	NC	NC
Kansas–Oklahoma	0	0	0	0	0	NC	NC	NC
Kentucky–Missouri	11.976	10.390	10.203	15.071	16.176	17.899*	21.461*	23.350*
Kentucky–Ohio	0	0	0	NC	0	NC	NC	0*
Kentucky–Tennessee	11.976	10.390	10.203	NC	NC	NP	NP	NP
Kentucky–Virginia	0	0	0	NC	NC	NP	NP	NP
Kentucky–West Virginia	0	0	0	NC	NC	NP	NP	NP
Louisiana–Mississippi	11.976	10.390	10.203	NC	NC	17.899*	21.461*	23.350*
Louisiana–Texas	0	0	0	0	0	0*	0*	0*
Maine–New Hampshire	1.932	5.393	10.203	15.071*	16.176*	17.899*	21.461*	23.350*
Maryland–Pennsylvania	3.175	7.482	0	NC	NC	NP	NP	NP
Maryland–Virginia	12.834	19.765	10.203	NC	NC	NP	NP	NP
Maryland–West Virginia	12.834	19.765	10.203	NC	NC	NP	NP	NP
Maryland–District of Columbia	26.347	32.208	0	NC	NC	NP	NP	NP
Massachusetts–New Hampshire	0	0	14.527	15.071*	16.176*	17.899*	21.461*	23.350*
Massachusetts–New York	0	0	0	NC	NC	NC	NC	NC
Massachusetts–Rhode Island	0	0	3.775	15.592*	16.576*	18.074*	21.034*	22.535*
Massachusetts–Vermont	0	0	14.527	15.071*	16.176*	17.899*	21.461*	23.350*
Michigan–Ohio	11.976	10.390	8.514	34.496	62.176	NC	NC	157.746*
Minnesota–North Dakota	11.976	10.390	10.203	15.071	16.176	17.899*	21.461*	23.350*
Minnesota–South Dakota	11.976	10.390	10.203	15.071	16.176	NC	21.461*	23.350*
Minnesota–Wisconsin	8.982	3.896	0.609	NC'	NC	NP	NP	NP
Mississippi–Tennessee	0	0	0	NP	NP	NP	NP	NP
Missouri–Nebraska	11.976	10.390	4.836	5.026	5.415	6.027	7.313	8.009*
Missouri–Oklahoma	11.976	10.390	10.203	15.071	16.176	17.899*	21.461*	23.350*
Missouri–Tennessee	0	0	0	NC	NC	NP	NP	NP
Montana–North Dakota	0	0	2.411	6.651	7.101	NC	9.187*	9.907*
Montana–South Dakota	0	0	2.411	6.651	7.101	7.793	9.187*	9.907*
Montana–Wyoming	0	4.706	6.428	6.651	7.101	7.793	9.187*	9.907*
Nebraska–South Dakota	0	0	15.533	20.855	22.467	NC	30.344*	33.228*
Nebraska–Wyoming	0	4.706	20.065	20.855	22.467	NC	30.344*	33.228*

(continued)

99

(Table 4.12 continued)

Percentage Productivity Loss by Vehicle Axle Code Classification

Two-State Route	2-S1	2-S2	3-S2	2-S1-2	3-S1-2	3-S2-2	3-S2-3	3-S2-4
Nevada–Oregon	0	0	0	19.489	49.728	57.610	67.047	71.831
Nevada–Utah	0	4.706	7.846	15.377	16.348	17.825	20.745	22.225
New Hampshire–Vermont	0	0	0	0*	0*	0*	0*	0*
New Jersey–New York	5.308	6.734	7.195	NC	NC	NC	NC	NC
New Jersey–Pennsylvania	2.067	7.758	10.203	NP	NP	NP	NP	NP
New Mexico–Oklahoma	8.556	4.518	1.255	12.473	13.261	14.459*	16.827*	18.028*
New Mexico–Texas	8.556	4.518	1.255	12.473	13.261	14.459*	16.827*	18.028*
New Mexico–Utah	8.556	7.378	6.509	2.582	2.726	NC	NC	NC
New York–Pennsylvania	3.175	3.731	14.527	NC	NC	NC	NC	NC
New York–Vermont	0	0	14.527	NC	NC	NC	NC	NC
North Carolina–South Carolina	10.695	4.494	1.531	1.581*	1.681*	1.834*	2.136*	2.289*
North Carolina–Tennessee	11.976	15.584	14.094	14.622*	15.695*	17.367*	20.822*	22.659*
North Carolina–Virginia	0	4.706	3.531	0*	0*	0*	0*	0*
North Dakota–South Dakota	0	0	0	0	0	NC	NC	0*
Ohio–Pennsylvania	16.417	14.471	18.450	NC	NC	NC	NC	NP
Ohio–West Virginia	0	0	0	NC	NC	NC	NC	NP
Oklahoma–Texas	0	0	0	0	0	0*	0*	0*
Oregon–Washington	0	0	4.083	29.592*	63.258	NC	NC	NC
Pennsylvania–West Virginia	16.417	14.471	18.450	15.071*	16.176*	17.899*	21.461*	23.350*
South Dakota–Wyoming	0	4.706	3.923	0	0	0	0*	0*
Tennessee–Virginia	11.976	10.390	10.203	14.622*	15.695*	17.367*	20.822*	22.655*
Utah–Wyoming	0	0	3.775	15.377	16.348	17.825	NC	NC
Virginia–West Virginia	0	0	0	0.391*	0.416*	0.454*	0.529*	0.567*
Virginia–District of Columbia	11.976	10.390	10.203	14.622*	15.695*	17.367*	20.822*	22.655*

*Combination not permitted in either state. Percentage loss based on difference in payload between states as if vehicle were permitted.

Note: NC = not calculated because combination is permitted in one state but not the other state; NP = combination is prohibited in one state and length limitation is exceeded in the other state.

Source: Compiled by the authors.

TABLE 4.13

Percentage Productivity Loss Due to Restrictive Covenants in Weight Maximums on the Noninterstate Highway System for All Two-State Route Combinations

Two-State Route	Percentage Productivity Loss by Vehicle Axle Code Classification							
	2–S1	2–S2	3–S2	2–S1–2	3–S1–2	3–S2–2	3–S2–3	3–S2–4
Alabama–Florida	0	0	23.405	24.167*	25.693*	28.014*	32.603*	34.930*
Alabama–Georgia	8.718	10.057	23.405	NP	NP	NP	NP	NP
Alabama–Mississippi	23.952	41.558	41.332	NP	NP	NP	NP	NP
Alabama–Tennessee	23.952	41.558	41.332	42.880*	46.025*	50.928*	61.061*	66.435*
Arizona–California	0	0	0	0	0	0*	0*	0*
Arizona–Colorado	11.976	9.877	7.846	15.372	10.360	11.296*	13.146*	14.085*
Arizona–Nevada	0	0	0	19.489	49.728	NC	NC	NC
Arizona–New Mexico	8.556	4.518	1.255	12.473	13.261	14.459*	16.827*	18.028*
Arizona–Utah	0	4.706	7.846	15.377	16.348	NC	NC	NC
Arkansas–Louisiana	11.976	10.390	10.203	15.071	16.176	17.899*	21.461*	23.350*
Arkansas–Mississippi	0	0	0	NC	NC	0*	0*	0*
Arkansas–Missouri	0	0	0	0	0	0*	0*	0*
Arkansas–Oklahoma	11.976	10.390	10.203	15.071	16.176	17.899*	21.461*	23.350*
Arkansas–Tennessee	0	0	0	NC	NC	NP	NP	NP
Arkansas–Texas	11.976	10.390	10.203	15.071	16.176	17.899*	21.461*	23.350*
California–Nevada	0	0	0	19.489	49.728	NC	NC	NC
California–Oregon	0	0	0	19.489	49.728	NC	NC	NC
Colorado–Kansas	11.976	9.412	7.846	6.565	0.939	NC	NC	NC
Colorado–Nebraska	11.976	9.412	7.846	15.007	18.775	20.299*	23.238*	24.691*
Colorado–New Mexico	21.557	12.935	6.509	8.254	2.628	2.843*	3.253*	3.457*
Colorado–Oklahoma	11.976	9.412	7.846	15.372	10.360	11.296*	13.146*	14.085*
Colorado–Utah	11.976	4.706	0	11.049	5.426	NC	NC	NC
Colorado–Wyoming	11.976	4.706	0	15.007	30.040	NC	37.181*	39.506*
Connecticut–Massachusetts	2.123	2.490	15.224	15.798*	16.964*	18.785*	22.557	24.561*

(continued)

(Table 4.13 continued)

Percentage Productivity Loss by Vehicle Axle Code Classification

Two-State Route	2-S1	2-S2	3-S2	2-S1-2	3-S1-2	3-S2-2	3-S2-3	3-S2-4
Connecticut–New York	2.123	2.490	15.224	NC	NC	NC	NC	NC
Connecticut–Rhode Island	2.123	2.490	25.325	33.640*	36.107*	39.354*	47.903*	52.120*
Delaware–Maryland	12.834	16.360	0	0	0	0*	0*	0*
Delaware–New Jersey	18.824	8.539	16.364	NC	NC	20.164*	24.175*	26.303*
Delaware–Pennsylvania	16.417	9.326	0	NC	NC	NP	NP	NP
Florida–Georgia	8.718	10.057	0	NP	NP	NP	NP	NP
Georgia–North Carolina	1.818	6.495	0.379	NP	NP	NP	NP	NP
Georgia–South Carolina	8.718	5.508	1.148	NP	NP	NP	NP	NP
Georgia–Tennessee	14.012	28.623	14.527	NP	NP	NP	NC	88.854*
Idaho–Montana	0	0	2.411	27.437	60.360	69.893	92.441	NC
Idaho–Nevada	0	0	2.411	27.437	60.360	78.416	82.393	NC
Idaho–Oregon	0	0	2.411	27.437	60.360	69.893	31.838	NC
Idaho–Utah	0	4.706	10.446	23.051	24.610	27.007	NC	2.540*
Idaho–Washington	0	0	1.633	1.691	1.807	NC	NC	NC
Idaho–Wyoming	0	4.706	10.446	27.437	53.703	58.934	NC	188.047*
Illinois–Indiana	0	0	1.556	19.556	54.690	NC	0*	0*
Illinois–Iowa	3.234	3.896	0	NC	NC	0*	0*	30.299*
Illinois–Kentucky	17.964	17.403	17.533	19.556	20.990	23.227*	27.848*	0*
Illinois–Missouri	0	0	0	0	0	0*	0*	NP
Illinois–Wisconsin	8.982	3.896	0.609	NC	NC	NP	NP	121.067*
Indiana–Kentucky	17.964	17.403	17.553	45.020	72.883	NC	NC	10.374*
Indiana–Michigan	0	0	0	0	NC	NC	NC	133.521*
Indiana–Ohio	11.976	10.390	8.514	34.496	62.176	96.623	128.773	0*
Iowa–Minnesota	3.234	3.896	0	NC	NC	0*	0*	0*
Iowa–Missouri	3.234	3.896	0	NC	NC	0*	0*	0*
Iowa–Nebraska	8.469	6.250	10.203	NC	NC	57.854*	69.364*	75.469*
Iowa–South Dakota	8.469	6.250	10.203	NC	NC	NC	69.364*	75.469*
Iowa–Wisconsin	5.568	4.800	0.609	NP	NP	NP	NP	NP

Kansas–Missouri	11.976	10.390	10.203	27.405	29.415	NC	NC	NC
Kansas–Nebraska	0	0	0	7.921	17.670	NC	NC	NC
Kansas–Oklahoma	0	0	0	10.719	11.396	NC	NC	NC
Kentucky–Missouri	17.964	17.403	17.553	19.556	20.990	23.227*	27.848*	30.299*
Kentucky–Ohio	5.348	6.353	6.669	3.898	4.114	NC	NC	5.634*
Kentucky–Tennessee	17.964	17.403	17.553	NC	NC	NP	NP	NP
Kentucky–Virginia	5.348	0	3.031	NC	NC	NP	NP	NP
Kentucky–West Virginia	11.976	6.353	6.669	NC	NC	NP	NP	NP
Louisiana–Mississippi	11.976	10.390	10.203	NC	NC	17.899*	21.461*	23.350*
Louisiana–Texas	0	0	0	0	0	0*	0*	0*
Maine–New Hampshire	1.932	5.161	14.527	15.071*	16.176*	17.899*	21.461*	23.350*
Maryland–Pennsylvania	3.175	7.920	0	NC	NC	NP	NP	NP
Maryland–Virginia	7.107	14.558	14.094	NC	NC	NP	NP	NP
Maryland–West Virginia	12.834	22.349	18.450	NC	NC	NP	NP	NP
Maryland–District of Columbia	1.932	6.763	0	NC	NC	NP	NP	NP
Massachusetts–New Hampshire	0	0	14.527	15.071*	16.176*	17.899*	21.461*	23.350*
Massachusetts–New York	0	0	0	0	NC	NC	NC	NC
Massachusetts–Rhode Island	0	0	3.775	15.592*	16.576*	18.074*	21.034*	22.535
Massachusetts–Vermont	0	0	14.527	15.071*	16.176*	17.899*	21.461*	23.350*
Michigan–Ohio	11.976	10.390	8.514	34.496	62.176	NC	NC	157.746*
Minnesota–North Dakota	11.976	10.390	10.203	15.071	16.176	17.899*	21.461*	23.350*
Minnesota–South Dakota	11.976	10.390	10.203	37.497	52.283	NC	69.364*	75.469*
Minnesota–Wisconsin	8.982	3.896	0.609	NC	NC	NP	NP	NP
Mississippi–Tennessee	0	0	0	NP	NP	NP	NP	NP
Missouri–Nebraska	11.976	10.390	10.203	37.497	52.283	57.854*	69.364*	75.469*
Missouri–Oklahoma	11.976	10.390	10.203	15.071	16.176	17.899*	21.461*	23.350*
Missouri–Tennessee	0	0	0	NC	NC	NP	NP	NP
Montana–North Dakota	0	0	0	19.489	49.728	NC	67.047*	71.831*
Montana–South Dakota	0	0	0	0	14.226	17.718	19.799*	20.792*
Montana–Wyoming	0	4.706	7.846	0	8.573	6.895	7.623*	7.965*
Nebraska–South Dakota	0	0	0	0	0	NC	0*	0*
Nebraska–Wyoming	0	4.706	7.846	0	9.484	NC	11.314*	11.881*

(continued)

(Table 4.13 continued)

Percentage Productivity Loss by Vehicle Axle Code Classification

Two-State Route	2-S1	2-S2	3-S2	2-S1-2	3-S1-2	3-S2-2	3-S2-3	3-S2-4
Nevada–Oregon	0	0	0	0	0	5.017	5.509	5.738
Nevada–Utah	0	4.706	7.846	3.564	35.019	40.477	45.968	48.652
New Hampshire–Vermont	0	0	0	0*	0*	0*	0*	0*
New Jersey–New York	5.308	3.017	1.604	NC	NC	NC	NC	NC
New Jersey–Pennsylvania	2.067	3.871	16.364	NP	NP	NP	NP	NP
New Mexico–Oklahoma	8.556	4.518	1.255	12.473	13.261	14.459*	16.827*	18.028*
New Mexico–Texas	8.556	4.518	1.255	12.473	13.261	14.459*	16.827*	18.028*
New Mexico–Utah	8.556	7.378	6.509	2.582	2.726	NC	NC	NC
New York–Pennsylvania	3.175	3.731	14.527	NC	NC	NC	NC	NC
New York–Vermont	0	0	14.527	NC	NC	NC	NC	NC
North Carolina–South Carolina	10.695	7.742	1.531	1.581*	1.681*	1.834*	2.136*	2.289*
North Carolina–Tennessee	11.976	20.779	14.094	14.622*	15.695*	17.367*	20.822*	22.655*
North Carolina–Virginia	5.348	7.466	0	0*	0*	0*	0*	0*
North Dakota–South Dakota	0	0	0	19.489	31.080	NC	39.439*	42.254*
Ohio–Pennsylvania	16.417	14.471	18.450	NC	NC	NC	NC	NP
Ohio–West Virginia	0	0	0	NC	NC	NC	NC	NP
Oklahoma–Texas	0	0	0	0	0	0*	0*	0*
Oregon–Washington	0	0	4.083	29.592	63.258	NC	NC	NC
Pennsylvania–West Virginia	16.417	14.471	18.450	15.071*	16.176*	17.899*	21.461*	23.350*
South Dakota–Wyoming	0	4.706	7.846	0	9.484	10.124	11.314*	11.881*
Tennessee–Virginia	17.964	17.403	14.094	14.622*	15.695*	17.367*	20.822*	22.655*
Utah–Wyoming	0	0	0	3.564	23.347	25.138	NC	NC
Virginia–West Virginia	5.348	6.353	3.531	0.391*	0.416*	0.454*	0.529*	0.567*
Virginia–District of Columbia	5.076	7.301	14.094	14.622*	15.695*	17.367*	20.822*	22.655*

*Combination not permitted in either state. Percentage loss based on difference in payload between states as if vehicle were permitted.

Note: NC = not calculated because combination is permitted in one state but not the other state; NP = combination is prohibited in one state and length limitation is exceeded in the other state.

Source: Compiled by the authors.

combination. This particular axle-code classification was chosen for two distinct reasons: first, it was a permissible combination in all states; and second, aside from the front axle, one single axle and one tandem axle were possessed, thus insuring that both a state's single- and tandem-axle restrictions could be tested. The selection of the noninterstate system was made in order that all states would be embodied in the simulation. (Alaska has no interstate network.) The outcome of this undertaking is displayed in Tables 4.14, 4.15, and 4.16, which reveal respectively the productivity change associated with a universal single-axle limitation of 22 kips; a universal tandem-axle restriction of 38 kips; and the total effect of both limitations when imposed simultaneously.

Validation of the Model

Validating a model basically involves resolving two inquiries: does the model adequately portray the real-world system and, if so, does it produce results representative of this system? The response to the initial inquiry is a function of the accuracy of state size and weight data and truck data. Because of the constant, ongoing process of alteration of state statutes pertinent to weight and dimension regulations, the model must be presumed to be static. Given this assumption, accuracy then becomes a problem of interpretation. That is, the size factors in many states are subject to various exceptions and exemptions; in several states, the single- and tandem-axle restrictions include a statutory enforcement tolerance; and, finally, the gross-weight limitation throughout the United States can be calculated in three different ways.* The salient point is simply that any two individuals, groups, or organizations acting independently are unlikely to completely concur on the interpretation of size and weight maximums for the several states. Differences, however slight, can change payload and/or cubic capacity and, hence, productivity. Truck data, on the other hand, when existent, tends to be more uniform, the only difficulty, besides the arbitrary rounding of tare-weight figures, is normally manifested in dissimilar interior dimensions. Of course, either of these differences can cause variances in productivity computations. Therefore, model validation, in this case, centered on obtaining the most reasonable size, weight, and truck data.

The second question posed above addresses itself to the validation of the simulation proper. In this respect, the logic of the entire computer model

---

*The majority of states use a table; however, a significant number of states either use a formula or actually specify a numerical limitation.

TABLE 4.14

The Effect of Adopting the Winfrey Study Single-Axle Recommendation of 22 Kips for the 2–S2 Vehicle Axle Code Classification on the Noninterstate Highway System

State	Payload before Change in Pounds	Payload after Change in Pounds	Percent Change
Alabama	54,500	54,500	0
Alaska	42,500	44,500	+ 4.706
Arizona	42,500	44,500	+ 4.706
Arkansas	38,500	42,500	+10.390
California	42,500	44,500	+ 4.706
Colorado	42,500	46,500	+ 9.412
Connecticut	48,068	47,220	− 1.764
Delaware	44,500	46,500	+ 4.494
Florida	54,500	54,500	0
Georgia	49,520	51,180	+ 3.352
Hawaii	44,500	42,500	− 4.494
Idaho	42,500	44,500	+ 4.706
Illinois	38,500	42,500	+10.390
Indiana	38,500	42,500	+10.390
Iowa	40,000	43,460	+ 8.650
Kansas	42,500	44,500	+ 4.706
Kentucky	45,200	46,200	+ 2.212
Louisiana	42,500	44,500	+ 4.706
Maine	48,500	48,500	0
Maryland	51,780	51,500	− 0.541
Massachusetts	46,900	46,500	− 0.853
Michigan	38,500	42,500	+10.390
Minnesota	38,500	42,500	+10.390
Mississippi	38,500	42,500	+10.390
Missouri	38,500	42,500	+10.390
Montana	42,500	44,500	+ 4.706
Nebraska	42,500	44,500	+ 4.706
Nevada	42,500	44,500	+ 4.706
New Hampshire	46,900	46,500	− 0.853
New Jersey	47,720	46,200	− 3.185
New Mexico	44,420	44,820	+ 0.900
New York	46,900	46,500	− 0.853
North Carolina	46,500	48,500	+ 4.301
North Dakota	42,500	44,500	+ 4.706
Ohio	42,500	44,500	+ 4.706
Oklahoma	42,500	44,500	+ 4.706
Oregon	42,500	44,500	+ 4.706
Pennsylvania	48,650	47,580	− 2.199
Rhode Island	46,900	46,500	− 0.853
South Carolina	50,100	50,100	0
South Dakota	42,500	44,500	+ 4.706
Tennessee	38,500	42,500	+10.390
Texas	42,500	44,500	+ 4.706
Utah	44,500	46,500	+ 4.494
Vermont	46,900	46,500	− 0.853
Virginia	45,200	46,500	+ 2.212
Washington	42,500	44,500	+ 4.706
West Virginia	42,500	44,500	+ 4.706
Wisconsin	40,000	42,500	+ 6.250
Wyoming	44,500	46,500	+ 4.494
District of Columbia	48,500	48,500	0

Source: Compiled by the authors.

TABLE 4.15

The Effect of Adopting the Winfrey Study Tandem-Axle
Recommendation of 38 Kips for the 2–S2 Vehicle Axle Code
Classification on the Noninterstate Highway System

State	Payload before Change in Pounds	Payload after Change in Pounds	Percent Change
Alabama	54,500	48,500	−11.009
Alaska	42,500	46,500	+ 9.412
Arizona	42,500	46,500	+ 9.412
Arkansas	38,500	44,500	+15.584
California	42,500	46,500	+ 9.412
Colorado	42,500	44,500	+ 4.706
Connecticut	48,068	49,348	+ 2.663
Delaware	44,500	46,500	+ 4.494
Florida	54,500	44,500	−18.349
Georgia	49,520	46,840	− 5.412
Hawaii	44,500	50,500	+13.483
Idaho	42,500	46,500	+ 9.412
Illinois	38,500	44,500	+15.584
Indiana	38,500	44,500	+15.584
Iowa	40,000	44,040	+12.600
Kansas	42,500	46,500	+ 9.412
Kentucky	45,200	46,500	+ 4.425
Louisiana	42,500	46,500	+ 9.412
Maine	48,500	48,500	0
Maryland	51,780	48,900	− 5.562
Massachusetts	46,900	48,900	+ 4.264
Michigan	38,500	44,500	+15.584
Minnesota	38,500	44,500	+15.584
Mississippi	38,500	44,500	+15.584
Missouri	38,500	44,500	+15.584
Montana	42,500	46,500	+ 9.412
Nebraska	42,500	46,500	+ 9.412
Nevada	42,500	46,500	+ 9.412
New Hampshire	46,900	48,900	+ 4.264
New Jersey	47,720	50,020	+ 4.820
New Mexico	44,420	48,100	+ 8.285
New York	46,900	48,900	+ 4.264
North Carolina	46,500	46,500	0
North Dakota	42,500	46,500	+ 9.412
Ohio	42,500	46,500	+ 9.412
Oklahoma	42,500	46,500	+ 9.412
Oregon	42,500	46,500	+ 9.412
Pennsylvania	48,650	49,570	+ 1.891
Rhode Island	46,900	48,900	+ 4.264
South Carolina	50,100	48,500	− 3.194
South Dakota	42,500	46,500	+ 9.412
Tennessee	38,500	44,500	+15.584
Texas	42,500	46,500	+ 9.412
Utah	44,500	46,500	+ 4.494
Vermont	46,900	48,900	+ 4.264
Virginia	45,200	47,500	+ 4.425
Washington	42,500	46,500	+ 9.412
West Virginia	42,500	46,500	+ 9.412
Wisconsin	40,000	46,000	+15.000
Wyoming	44,500	46,500	+ 4.494
District of Columbia	48,500	48,500	0

Source: Compiled by the authors.

TABLE 4.16

The Effect of Simultaneously Adopting the Winfrey Study Single/Tandem Axle Recommendations of 22/38 Kips for the 2-S2 Vehicle Axle Code Classification on the Noninterstate Highway System

State	Payload before Change in Pounds	Payload after Change in Pounds	Percent Change
Alabama	54,500	48,500	−11.009
Alaska	42,500	48,500	+14.118
Arizona	42,500	48,500	+14.118
Arkansas	38,500	48,500	+25.974
California	42,500	48,500	+14.118
Colorado	42,500	48,500	+14.118
Connecticut	48,068	48,500	+ 0.899
Delaware	44,500	48,500	+ 8.989
Florida	54,500	48,500	−11.009
Georgia	49,520	48,500	− 2.060
Hawaii	44,500	48,500	+ 8.989
Idaho	42,500	48,500	+14.118
Illinois	38,500	48,500	+25.974
Indiana	38,500	48,500	+25.974
Iowa	40,000	48,500	+21.250
Kansas	42,500	48,500	+14.118
Kentucky	45,200	48,500	+ 6.637
Louisiana	42,500	48,500	+14.118
Maine	48,500	48,500	0
Maryland	51,780	48,500	− 6.334
Massachusetts	46,900	48,500	+ 3.412
Michigan	38,500	48,500	+25.974
Minnesota	38,500	48,500	+25.974
Mississippi	38,500	48,500	+25.974
Missouri	38,500	48,500	+25.974
Montana	42,500	48,500	+14.118
Nebraska	42,500	48,500	+14.118
Nevada	42,500	48,500	+14.118
New Hampshire	46,900	48,500	+ 3.412
New Jersey	47,720	48,500	+ 1.635
New Mexico	44,420	48,500	+ 9.185
New York	46,900	48,500	+ 3.412
North Carolina	46,500	48,500	+ 4.301
North Dakota	42,500	48,500	+14.118
Ohio	42,500	48,500	+14.118
Oklahoma	42,500	48,500	+14.118
Oregon	42,500	48,500	+14.118
Pennsylvania	48,650	48,500	− 0.308
Rhode Island	46,900	48,500	+ 3.412
South Carolina	50,100	48,500	− 3.194
South Dakota	42,500	48,500	+14.118
Tennessee	38,500	48,500	+25.974
Texas	42,500	48,500	+14.118
Utah	44,500	48,500	+ 8.989
Vermont	46,900	48,500	+ 3.412
Virginia	45,200	48,500	+ 7.301
Washington	42,500	48,500	+14.118
West Virginia	42,500	48,500	+14.118
Wisconsin	40,000	48,500	+21.250
Wyoming	44,500	48,500	+ 8.989
District of Columbia	48,500	48,500	0

Source: Compiled by the authors.

TABLE 4.17

Validation of the Simulation Model

Route Configuration	Vehicle Type	Highway System	Payload, in Pounds		Percent Loss		Cubic Capacity, in Cubic Feet		Percent Loss	
			Maximum	Minimum	Actual	Computed	Maximum	Minimum	Actual	Computed
Delaware–Maryland	2–S1	noninterstate	42,200	37,400	12.834	12.834	2272.1	2272.1	0	0
Michigan–Ohio	2–S2	interstate	42,500	38,500	10.390	10.390	2599.8	2599.8	0	0
Arkansas–Texas	3–S2	noninterstate	50,980	46,260	10.203	10.203	3582.8	2927.4	22.388	22.390
Kentucky–Missouri	2–S1–2	interstate	51,310	44,590	15.071	15.071	3495.6	3495.6	0	0
Colorado–Nebraska	3–S1–2	noninterstate	63,263	53,263	18.775	18.775	3495.6	3495.6	0	0
Montana–Wyoming	3–S2–2	interstate	44,263	41,063	7.793	7.793	5189.7	4282.4	21.187	21.187
Idaho–Utah	3–S2–3	noninterstate	45,923	34,833	31.838	31.838	6191.9	5199.5	19.086	19.088
Nevada–Oregon	3–S2–4	interstate	61,000	35,500	71.831	71.831	6199.3	5854.9	5.882	5.882

Source: Compiled by the authors.

TABLE 4.18

Summary of Productivity Loss Due to Restrictive Covenants in Size Maximums on Interstate and Noninterstate Highway Systems for Various Vehicle Axle Code Classifications on All Two-State Route Configurations

Vehicle Combination Classification

Percentage Loss	2-S1 Interstate Number	Percent	2-S1 Noninterstate Number	Percent	2-S2 Interstate Number	Percent	2-S2 Noninterstate Number	Percent	3-S2 Interstate Number	Percent	3-S2 Noninterstate Number	Percent	2-S1-2 Interstate Number	Percent	2-S1-2 Noninterstate Number	Percent
0	85	79	78	72	85	79	78	72	61	56	59	55	30	28	28	26
0.001- 6.0	13	12	8	7	13	12	8	7	5	5	3	3	5	5	4	4
6.001- 12.0	10	9	17	16	10	9	17	16	20	19	22	20	7	6	8	7
12.001- 18.0	—*	—	5	5	—	—	5	5	2	2	3	3	—	—	2	2
18.001- 24.0	—	—	—	—	—	—	—	—	13	12	11	10	22	20	19	18
24.001- 30.0	—	—	—	—	—	—	—	—	3	3	5	5	5	5	5	5
30.001- 40.0	—	—	—	—	—	—	—	—	4	4	3	3	3	3	1	1
40.001- 50.0	—	—	—	—	—	—	—	—	—	—	2	2	—	—	—	—
50.001- 60.0	—	—	—	—	—	—	—	—	—	—	—	—	—	—	—	—
60.001- 70.0	—	—	—	—	—	—	—	—	—	—	—	—	—	—	—	—
70.001- 80.0	—	—	—	—	—	—	—	—	—	—	—	—	—	—	—	—
80.001- 90.0	—	—	—	—	—	—	—	—	—	—	—	—	—	—	—	—
90.001-100.0	—	—	—	—	—	—	—	—	—	—	—	—	—	—	—	—
100+	—	—	—	—	—	—	—	—	—	—	—	—	—	—	—	—
NP	—	—	—	—	—	—	—	—	—	—	—	—	9	8	9	8
NC	—	—	—	—	—	—	—	—	—	—	—	—	27	25	27	25

	3-S1-2				3-S2-2				3-S2-3				3-S2-4			
	Interstate		Noninterstate		Interstate		Noninterstate		Interstate		Noninterstate		Interstate		Noninterstate	
Percentage Loss	Number	Percent	Number	Percent	Number	Percent	Number	Percent	Number	Percent	Number	Percent	Number	Percent	Number	Percent
0	30	28	28	26	1	1	1	1	1	1	1	1	—	—	—	—
0.001– 6.0	5	5	4	4	2	2	2	2	2	2	2	2	2	2	2	2
6.001– 12.0	7	6	8	7	2	2	—	—	1	1	1	1	—	—	8	7
12.001– 18.0	—	—	2	2	3	3	2	2	2	2	12	11	8	7	—	—
18.001– 24.0	22	20	19	18	29	27	32	30	10	9	—	—	—	—	10	9
24.001– 30.0	5	5	5	5	1	1	1	1	—	—	—	—	10	9	—	—
30.001– 40.0	3	3	5	5	1	1	1	1	—	—	—	—	—	—	—	—
40.001– 50.0	—	—	1	1	16	15	16	15	28	26	28	26	28	26	28	26
50.001– 60.0	—	—	—	—	1	1	1	1	—	—	—	—	—	—	—	—
60.001– 70.0	—	—	—	—	—	—	—	—	—	—	—	—	—	—	—	—
70.001– 80.0	—	—	—	—	—	—	—	—	16	15	16	15	—	—	—	—
80.001– 90.0	—	—	—	—	—	—	—	—	—	—	—	—	—	—	—	—
90.001–100.0	—	—	—	—	—	—	—	—	—	—	—	—	16	15	16	15
100+	—	—	—	—	—	—	—	—	—	—	—	—	—	—	—	—
NP	9	8	9	8	21	19	21	19	21	19	21	19	23	21	23	21
NC	27	25	27	25	31	29	31	29	27	25	27	25	21	19	21	19

*Dashes indicate category not applicable.

Note: Percentages may not add to 100 due to rounding. NP = not permitted; NC = not calculated.

Source: Compiled by the authors.

TABLE 4.19

Summary of Productivity Loss Due to Restrictive Covenants in Weight Maximums on Interstate and Noninterstate Highway Systems for Various Vehicle Axle Code Classifications on All Two-State Route Configurations

Vehicle Combination Classification

Percentage Loss	2-S1 Interstate		2-S1 Noninterstate		2-S2 Interstate		2-S2 Noninterstate		3-S2 Interstate		3-S2 Noninterstate		2-S1-2 Interstate		2-S1-2 Noninterstate	
	Number	Percent	Number	Percent	Number	Percent	Number	Percent	Number	Percent	Number	Percent	Number	Percent	Number	Percent
0	52	48	43	40	40	37	36	33	35	32	35	32	22	20	15	14
0.001- 6.0	14	13	19	18	28	26	26	24	27	25	19	18	5	5	7	6
6.001- 12.0	33	31	31	29	29	27	31	29	28	26	28	26	5	5	5	5
12.001- 18.0	7	6	11	10	6	6	10	9	13	12	18	17	28	26	22	20
18.001- 24.0	1	1	4	4	2	2	2	2	4	4	5	5	8	7	9	8
24.001- 30.0	1	1	—	—	3	3	1	1	1	1	1	1	2	2	7	6
30.001- 40.0	—	—	—	—	—	—	—	—	—	—	—	—	2	2	5	5
40.001- 50.0	—	—	—	—	—	—	2	2	—	—	2	2	—	—	2	2
50.001- 60.0	—	—	—	—	—	—	—	—	—	—	—	—	—	—	—	—
60.001- 70.0	—	—	—	—	—	—	—	—	—	—	—	—	—	—	—	—
70.001- 80.0	—	—	—	—	—	—	—	—	—	—	—	—	—	—	—	—
80.001- 90.0	—	—	—	—	—	—	—	—	—	—	—	—	—	—	—	—
90.001-100.0	—	—	—	—	—	—	—	—	—	—	—	—	—	—	—	—
100+	—	—	—	—	—	—	—	—	—	—	—	—	—	—	—	—
NP	—	—	—	—	—	—	—	—	—	—	—	—	9	8	9	8
NC	—	—	—	—	—	—	—	—	—	—	—	—	27	25	27	25

	3-S1-2				3-S2-2				3-S2-3				3-S2-4			
	Interstate		Noninterstate		Interstate		Noninterstate		Interstate		Noninterstate		Interstate		Noninterstate	
Percentage Loss	Number	Percent	Number	Percent	Number	Percent	Number	Percent	Number	Percent	Number	Percent	Number	Percent	Number	Percent
0	22	20	11	10	18	17	12	11	19	18	13	12	22	20	12	12
0.001- 6.0	5	5	8	7	2	2	4	4	2	2	4	4	3	3	6	6
6.001- 12.0	5	5	6	6	6	6	4	4	6	6	3	3	5	5	4	4
12.001- 18.0	28	26	20	19	22	20	17	16	4	4	5	5	—*	—	2	2
18.001- 24.0	4	4	4	4	3	3	6	6	21	19	17	19	25	23	18	17
24.001- 30.0	1	1	3	3	2	2	3	3	1	1	3	3	2	2	3	3
30.001- 40.0	1	1	4	4	1	1	1	1	4	4	4	4	3	3	4	4
40.001- 50.0	2	2	5	5	—	—	1	1	1	1	2	2	1	1	2	2
50.001- 60.0	1	1	4	4	1	1	4	4	—	—	—	—	—	—	1	1
60.001- 70.0	3	3	6	6	1	1	2	2	—	—	6	6	1	1	1	1
70.001- 80.0	—	—	1	1	—	—	1	1	1	1	—	—	1	1	5	5
80.001- 90.0	—	—	—	—	—	—	—	—	—	—	1	1	—	—	1	1
90.001-100.0	—	—	—	—	—	—	1	1	—	—	1	1	—	—	—	—
100+	—	—	—	—	—	—	—	—	—	—	1	1	2	2	4	4
NP	9	8	9	8	21	19	21	19	21	19	21	19	23	21	23	21
NC	27	25	27	25	31	29	31	29	27	25	27	25	21	19	21	19

*Dashes indicate category not applicable.

Note: Percentages may not add to 100 due to rounding. NP = not permitted; NC = not calculated.

Source: Compiled by the authors.

had to be tested. A portion of this test is displayed in Table 4.17. Eight two-state route combinations were selected representing the eight vehicle types and both the interstate and noninterstate highway systems. For each route both forms of productivity loss were computed and compared with the results obtained from the actual computer simulation. The maximum deviation from the percentages presented in Tables 4.10 through 4.13 was .002. Therefore, the computer model yielded results that were quite consistent with the real-world system.

Analysis of the Simulation Results

The results obtained in the firm segment of the model are summarized in Tables 4.18 and 4.19. These tables contain data that categorize the productivity loss due to restrictive covenants in size and weight maximums on the interstate and noninterstate highway systems for all vehicles utilized in the study on all two-state route configurations. It is not surprising that Table 4.19, which pertains to the weight factors, clearly exhibits a wider margin of disparity for most vehicles than those results shown for the size elements in Table 4.18. This disparity can be explained by recalling from Chapter 3 that the size factors of width and height are relatively uniform throughout the Unites States. This disparity can be further illustrated by examining the number of route combinations for each vehicle that exceed a 6 percent loss in productivity and by establishing a range for the size and weight categories. Table 4.20 discloses that for the eight vehicle types included in the study an average of 36 percent of all two-state interstate route combinations showed a loss in productivity greater than 6 percent due to size factors; on the noninterstate system the arithmetic mean was 43 routes or 40 percent of the 108 possible configurations.

TABLE 4.20

Minimum and Maximum Number and Percentage of
Two-State Routes That Exceed a Six Percent Loss in Productivity

Category and Highway System	Minimum		Maximum		Arithmetic Mean	
	Number	Percent	Number	Percent	Number	Percent
Size						
Interstate	10	9	62	57	39	36
Noninterstate	22	20	62	57	43	40
Weight						
Interstate	36	33	46	43	42	39
Noninterstate	40	37	54	50	47	44

Source: Compiled by the authors.

Albeit the weight factors had a much more compact range between smallest and largest number of two-state routes with a greater than 6 percent loss in productivity, they imparted averages comparable to those found for the size elements. These were 42 (39 percent) and 47 (44 percent two-state routes for the interstate and noninterstate highway systems, respectively.

The results procured from the government portion of the model are recapitulated in Table 4.21. This partial table groups the states by change in payload as a result of adopting the Winfrey Study's single- and tandem-axle recommendations for the 2-S2 vehicle axle-code classification on the noninterstate highway system. The 2-S2 combination would gain more than 6 percent in only 11 states (22 percent) if just the single-axle proposal of the Winfrey Study were endorsed; however, approval of the tandem-axle proposal solely or adoption of both recommendations simultaneously would increase the payload of the 2-S2 by more than 6 percent in 29 and 35 states respectively.

Even though the preceding analysis has concentrated on the productivity loss to motor carriers due to restrictive covenants in size and weight maximums and the conceivable change in productivity to a particular vehicle consequent to alteration of certain restrictions, this analysis contains ramifications that extend substantially far beyond productivity loss or gain alone. In the first place, productivity is directly tied to diesel-fuel consumption. To a trucking firm, increased productivity translates into fewer trips and, hence,

TABLE 4.21

Summary of Productivity Change in the United States as a Result of Adopting the Winfrey Study Single/Tandem Axle Recommendations of 22/38 Kips for the 2–S2 Vehicle Axle Code Classification on the Noninterstate Highway System

Change in Productivity	Single Axle		Tandem Axle		Single and Tandem Axles	
	Number of States	Percent	Number of States	Percent	Number of States	Percent
Decrease	10	20	5	10	6	12
No change	5	10	3	6	2	4
+ .001– 6.0	25	49	14	27	8	16
+ 6.00 –12.0	11	22	18	35	7	14
+12.001–18.0	—*	—	11	22	18	35
+18.001–24.0	—	—	—	—	2	4
+24.001–30.0	—	—	—	—	8	16

*Dashes indicate category not applicable.
Note: Percentages may not add up to 100 due to rounding.
Source: Compiled by the authors.

increased fuel efficiency. The precise amount of fuel savings depends upon the commodity density being transported, but a 1973 American Trucking Associations study revealed that substitution of twin trailers (2-S1-2 or 3-S1-2) for 55-foot tractor semitrailers (3-S2), in cases of light and bulky cargo, would reduce truck trips by between 30 and 44.5 percent while concurrently economizing on fuel consumption by 21.4 to 31.8 percent. Other comparisons using dense freight demonstrated savings ranging up to 16.5 percent fewer trips and 10.6 percent less fuel utilization.[6] Fewer trips can alter the wage-rate structure and ultimately mean a smaller investment in equipment. Investment in equipment can represent a substantial savings to the firm, as a typical tandem-axle road tractor ordered in 1973 and delivered in 1974 cost $6,522 (27.6 percent) more from the same supplier in 1975. This becomes even more significant when coupled with the expectation that tonnage by truck will double by 1990.[7]

The government unit faced with granting a productivity increase, ceteris paribus, would stand to suffer a reduction in tax revenue. However, this could be rectified simply by redistributing the current tax based upon alterations in the computed cost responsibilities of the various classes of highway users. Government units, vitally concerned with motor-vehicle safety, would also have to contend with the trade-off between less exposure to heavy trucks in general and the possible increased danger of having heavier trucks on the road.

For the firm that purchases transportation, productivity gains would meaningfully effect several of the micro-components of logistics. Aside from possibly diminishing transportation costs, greater productivity would reduce inventory carrying costs and ordering costs, and thus maintain the same customer service levels for a lower cost.[8]

NOTES

1. Claude McMillan and Richard F. Gonzalez, *Systems Analysis: A Computer Approach to Decision Models* (Homewood, Ill.: Richard D. Irwin, 1968), p. 23.

2. John McLeod, "Simulation Today—From Fuzz to Fact," *Simulation* 20 (March 1973): 9.

3. Robert C. Meier, William T. Newell, and Harold L. Pazer, *Simulation in Business and Economics* (Englewood Cliffs, N.J.: Prentice-Hall, 1969), p. 21.

4. Patricia G. Strauch, "Modeling in the Social Sciences: An Approach to Good Theory and Good Policy," *Simulation* 26 (January 1976): 155.

5. Leo P. Kadanoff, "From Simulation Model to Public Policy: An Examination of Forrester's 'Urban Dynamics,' " *Simulation* 16 (June 1971): 261.

6. Richard A. Staley, John L. Reith, and E. V. Kiley, "American Trucking and the Energy Crisis," Department of Research and Transport Economics, American Trucking Associations, April 1973, p. 4.

7. *1975 Motor Truck Facts* (New York: Motor Vehicle Manufacturers Association of the United States, 1975), pp. 3–4.

8. For an extended analysis of productivity and customer service levels consult Grant M. Davis and Stephen W. Brown, *Logistics Management* (Lexington, Mass.: D. C. Heath, 1975), chaps. 6–9.

CONCLUSIONS AND RECOMMENDATIONS

The basic thrust of this empirical investigation of the many problems associated with various state motor-carrier restrictive covenants was focused upon carrier productivity. Indeed, increasing productivity is a valid problem germane to the U.S. economy and the motor carrier is capable of a meaningful contribution. Because of certain institutional constraints, increasing state maximum weights and lengths to the standards prescribed by the federal government appears to be the optimal method for increasing carrier productivity.

Restrictive covenants exist in both motor-fuel taxation and size and weight maximums, which historically evolved as a direct result of incongruent state development prior to any federal participation. The lack of uniformity in the latter has been preserved by grandfather clauses contained in major federal size and weight legislation enacted by Congress during and since 1956. These major federal statutes have retarded productivity within the motor-carrier industry.

Although the Federal-Aid Highway Amendments of 1974 provided relief in all three weight categories for motor carriers operating on the interstate system, the basic impetus for these significant alterations was primarily motivated by energy considerations and the productivity loss that had occurred as a direct outgrowth of the 55-mph speed limit. Disregarding all factors except those crucial to an analysis of productivity, the purpose of this study was twofold. The first objective was to create a model capable of measuring the productivity loss directly attributable to restrictive covenants in size and weight maximums. The second purpose was to extend this model in order that a government unit might appraise the fiscal consequences of a conjectured modification in a size or weight standard.

To ascertain the magnitude of the trucking fleet potentially affected by maximum vehicle standards, together with the absolute volume of freight hauled by these vehicles, a previous investigation was concluded to be extremely conservative. In fact, over 7 million trucks (36.4 percent of all trucks and 5.95 percent of all vehicles) were estimated to conceivably be influenced by size and weight maximums. Moreover, these vehicles were calculated to have transported nearly 450 billion ton-miles of intercity freight in 1972. This represented 97.8 percent of the intercity freight ton-miles hauled by the motor-carrier industry and 21.7 percent of the total intercity freight ton-miles carried by all modes of transportation.

The available existing evidence regarding the extent to which greater cubic capacity and higher permissible weights could be utilized was considered moot. Cubic capacity is hindering more and more vehicles, perhaps as much as 50 percent of all shipments, as the trend toward lighter and bulkier freight continues. With respect to greater weight utilization, the fact that emerges is that a relatively small proportion of motor carriers, transporting a high percentage of total intercity tonnage, are reaping the benefits of weight maximums; moreover, there is a general concurrence that at least a majority of highway freight could profit from greater weights.

In addition to the interstate differentials in weight and dimension limitations, a substantial number of intrastate discrepancies exist. This development transpired because several states enacted legislation that authorized weights exceeding federal restrictions on certain designated highways. This legislative action created an anomalous situation whereby the interstate system, generally constructed to the highest possible engineering standards, was restricted to vehicles lighter than those tolerated on other roads. In all, 25 states have a minimum of one size or weight factor applicable to the noninterstate highway system that surpasses the allowable federal restriction on the interstate system.

The firm segment of the simulation model, which was utilized to test all 108 adjacent two-state route configurations, clearly demonstrated that the weight factors exhibited a wider range of disparity for most vehicles than the size elements. For the 8 vehicles analyzed in the model, an average of 39 interstate routes (36 percent) indicated a loss in productivity greater than 6 percent due to size factors; on the noninterstate system approximately 43 routes (40 percent) exhibited a loss in productivity beyond 6 percent. The weight factors exhibited similar averages and 47 routes (44 percent) on the interstate and noninterstate highway systems respectively.

In the government portion of the model, through analysis of the Winfrey Study single- and tandem-axle recommendations for the 2-S2 vehicle axle-code classification on the noninterstate highway system, 11 states (22 percent) would augment productivity by more than 6 percent through approbation of the single-axle recommendation. Endorsement of the tandem-axle limitation of 38,000 pounds would bolster productivity in 29 states (57 percent) by at least 6 percent. Simultaneous adoption of the two standards would increase productivity by at least 6 percent in 35 states (69 percent).

The implications of this study, moreover, extended far beyond productivity loss or gain alone. To the firm engaged in intercity trucking, productivity gains translate into fewer trips and increased fuel efficiency; this, in turn, can positively influence the wage-rate structure and investment in new equipment. On the other hand, the government unit granting a productivity augmentation must be concerned with the problems inherent in redistributing the current tax based upon new cost responsibilities. Finally, to the firm that purchases transportation, productivity increases influence-carrying costs, ordering costs, and customer-service levels.

Based on the information accumulated during the course of this investigation, four recommendations are proffered. First, grandfather provisions should be phased out of existing legislation and prohibited in future size and weight statutes. This analysis was lucidly demonstrated that the grandfather provision in the current law constitutes the primary force perpetuating underlying restrictive covenants in terms of both size and weight maximums. Removing this restrictive clause will institute legislative equality on the interstate system, which theoretically was built to the same standards throughout the United States. However, the decision to adopt maximum federal standards should be retained by the individual states.

Second, a nationwide classification of highways, extending beyond the current categorizations, should be conducted, with each highway receiving a rating based on national standards. The purpose of this action would essentially be twofold. First, a meaningful interstate comparison of highway quality would be allowed. In this regard, the federal government together with the states could establish an empirically justified size and weight range for each "grade" of highway. The latitude of this range would reflect all dimension of the size and weight field as well as such factors as fuel efficiency and geographical differences. Albeit each state could permissively select standards within the prescribed margin, differences throughout the United States would be predicated upon the specific grade of highway in lieu of the strength of the various lobbyists within the size and weight field. Second, the highway transportation system in the United States would be united and nationwide reciprocity in other highway-related areas, such as registration fees, motor-fuel taxation, and third-structure taxes, would be encouraged instead of the present state-by-state or regional reciprocity.

Third, twin-trailer operation (2-S1-2 and 3-S1-2) should be immediately sanctioned on the interstate highway system. Even though currently banned from operating in 16 states, the twin-trailer concept can increase cubic capacity by roughly one-third and gross vehicle weight by approximately 15 to 25 percent, depending, of course, upon commodity density. Furthermore, at a time when energy utilization is a vital national concern, twin trailers offer a 10- to 30-percent savings in fuel consumption. In adjacent two-state route configurations, twin trailers are prohibited in some manner from operating on

50 (46 percent) of the 108 combinations. On those routes where one state permits twin trailers and the other does not, the twins must be broken down or assembled at the allowing state's border, thus creating the necessity for excess manpower and equipment.

Fourth, oversize-overweight permit operation should be standardized and strictly enforced in the United States. the economical soundness of any transportation system is ultimately founded in a minimum number of retarding effects and the close scrutinization of loopholes. There is no question but that the public interest is best served if certain commodities in particular circumstances are transported in shipments that exceed existing maximum weight and dimension standards. However, judging from the diverse regulations of individual states, no current consensus on precisely what these commodities are has been established.

A final suggestion that could not be enacted through legislation is that the optimum density of the major vehicles engaged in intercity freight be calculated and consulted for determination of the optimal vehicle that can be utilized on a particular route configuration. The model developed in this study, for example, could be adapted to accommodate all types of vehicles owned and operated by a specific firm, and could thus ascertain a truck "mix" that would optimize the firm's resources.

This comprehensive analysis raises almost as many questions as it resolves. From Figure 1.1 the reader can readily infer that a host of factors pertinent to the size and weight area were either ignored or treated succinctly in this study. Some of the relationships, such as that between axle loadings and pavement life, are well documented by years of actual road-test conditions. Nevertheless, several of the highway cost studies need to be updated in view of the energy crisis and the permanent reduction in vehicle speeds. Other areas, particularly those related to social costs, are either currently being investigated or are under consideration for study. At present, a significant contribution could be made through a definitive study of combination-vehicle safety, particularly in accidents, with respect to type of vehicle involved, gross weight of vehicle, and cost of the accident in property and loss of future earnings.

This study has suggested that state loadometer surveys are not providing sufficient data to accurately determine the number of vehicles affected by maximum standards, nor the number of vehicles and/or tonnage being transported that could benefit from increased cubic capacity or additional weight allowance. Any of this information would be useful in obtaining a complete dimension of the significance of motor-carrier size and weight limitations.

Another area of exploration suggested by this analysis is the expansion of the simulation model to incorporate additional variables, such as other vehicle types, multilength cargo bodies, or other factors relevant to size and weight maximums. This could prove particularly beneficial if actual data from various sections of the United States were simulated to discover if a particular geographic region has less productivity loss than another and, if so, how this influences competition or concentration.

Finally, an important area not dealt with in this study and not apparent in Figure 1.1 is the effect of greater dimensions and weights on the diversion of goods from railroad to truck. Certainly any weight increase will enhance the competitive position of motor vehicles able to take advantage of such increases. Furthermore, a width increase to 102 inches might divert rail traffic that could be containerized. The real question of significance is to what extent increases in size and weight maximums influence national transportation policy.

Government Publications

State

Oregon. *General Laws.* 1919.

Federal

Bureau of Economics, Interstate Commerce Commission. *Transport Economics* 1, no. 4 (1974).

FHWA Task Force on Size and Weight Limitations of Trucks. "Effects of Increasing Truck Size and Weight on Highway Design to Accommodate Different Off-Tracking Characteristics." Interim Report. Mimeographed draft. February 21, 1975.

Hutchinson, B. M.; B. A. Sanders; and W. D. Glauz. *Effects of Current State Licensing, Permit, and Fee Requirements on Motor Trucks Involved in Interstate Commerce.* Washington, D.C.: Federal Highway Administration, Department of Transportation, 1975.

U.S. Bureau of the Census. Census of Transportation, 1972. *Truck Inventory and Use Survey: U.S. Summary, TC72-T52.* Washington, D.C.: Government Printing Office, 1973.

United States Code. 1970 ed. Washington, D.C.: Government Printing Office, 1971.

U.S. Congress. House. *Federal-Aid Highway and Highway Revenue Acts of 1956.* Conference Report, 84th Cong., 2d sess., 1956, H. Repts. 2022, 2436.

————. *Federal Regulation of Sizes and Weight of Motor Vehicles.* 77th Cong., 1st sess., 1941, H. Doc. 354.

————. *Maximum Desirable Dimensions and Weights of Vehicles Operated on the Federal-Aid Systems.* 88th Cong., 2d sess., 1964, H. Doc. 354.

U.S. Congress. House. Committee on Public Works. *Federal Highway and Highway Revenue Acts of 1956.* 84th Cong., 2d sess., 1956, H. Rept. 2022.

U.S. Congress. House. Committee on Public Works, Subcommittee on Roads. *Vehicle Weight and Dimension Limitations.* Hearing, 91st Cong., 1st sess., July 8–September 4, 1969.

U.S. Congress. House. Committee on Ways and Means. *Revenue Bill of 1918.* Report No. 767, 65th Cong., 2d sess., September 3, 1918.

U.S. Congress. Senate. Committee on Interstate and Foreign Commerce, Subcommittee on Domestic Land and Water Transportation. *Study of Domestic Land and Water Transportation.* Hearing, 81st Cong., 2d sess., April 4–July 28, 1950.

U.S. Congress. Senate. Committee on Public Works, Subcommittee on Roads. *Vehicle Sizes and Weights.* Hearing, 90th Cong., 2d sess., February 19–21 and March 7, 1968.

U.S. Congress. Senate. Committee on Public Works, Subcommittee on Transportation. *Transportation and the New Energy Policies (Truck Sizes and Weights)*. Part 2. Hearing, 93rd Cong., 2d sess., February 20–21 and March 26, 1974.

U.S. Congress. House. *Congressional Record*. 64th Cong., 1st sess., December 6, 1915-January 13, 1916, 53, pt. 1: 98.

U.S. Congress. *Congressional Record*. 90th Cong., 2d sess., July 24, 1968, 114, pt. 18: 23, 178–80.

U.S. Department of Labor. Bureau of Labor Statistics. *The Meaning and Measurement of Productivity*. Bulletin 1714. Washington, D.C.: Government Printing Office, 1971.

———. *Productivity and the Economy*. Bulletin 1779. Washington, D.C.: Government Printing Office, 1973.

U.S. Department of Transportation. Federal Highway Administration. "Effects of Increasing Truck Size and Weight on Increase in Freight Handling Capacity Per Truck Unit." Mimeographed draft. 1975.

———. *Highway Statistics, 1970*. Washington, D.C.: Government Printing Office, 1972.

———. *Highway Statistics, 1971*. Washington, D.C.: Government Printing Office, 1973.

———. *Highway Statistics, 1972*. Washington, D.C.: Government Printing Office, 1974.

———. *Highway Statistics, 1973*. Washington, D.C.: Government Printing Office, 1975.

———. "News." FHWA 94-75 (October 6, 1975).

———. *Review of Safety and Economic Aspects of Increased Vehicle Sizes and Weights*. Washington, D.C.: Federal Highway Administration, 1969.

———. *Road User and Property Taxes on Selected Motor Vehicles*. Washington, D.C.: Government Printing Office, 1973.

U.S. Department of Transportation. Federal Highway Administration. Bureau of Motor Carrier Safety. *Federal Motor Carrier Safety Regulations*. Title 49. Section 395.3. Washington, D.C.: Government Printing Office, October 1, 1974.

U.S. Department of Transportation. Federal Highway Administration. Bureau of Public Roads. *Highway Statistics, Summary to 1965*. Washington, D.C.: Government Printing Office, 1967.

———. *The Role of Third Structure Taxes in the Highway User Tax Family*. Washington, D.C.: Government Printing Office, 1968.

U.S. Public Roads Administration. *Highway Practice in the United States of America*. Washington, D.C.: Government Printing Office, 1949.

U.S. Public Roads Administration. Federal Works Agency. *Highway Statistics, Summary to 1945*. Washington, D.C.: Government Printing Office, 1947.

Winfrey, Robley et al. *Economics of the Maximum Limits of Motor Vehicle Dimensions and Weights.* 2 vols. Washington, D.C.: Federal Highway Administration, Department of Transportation, 1974.

Highway Research Board Publications

Highway Research Board. *Road Test One-MD, Final Report.* Special Report 4. Washington, D.C.: National Academy of Sciences-National Research Council, 1952.

————. *The AASHO Road Test, History and Description of Project.* Special Report 61A. Washington, D.C.: National Academy of Sciences-National Research Council, 1961.

————. *The AASHO Road Test, Proceedings of a Conference Held May 16–18, 1962, St. Louis, Mo.* Special Report 73. Washington, D.C.: National Academy of Sciences-National Research Council, 1962.

————. *The AASHO Road Test, Report 7, Summary Report.* Special Report 61G. Washington, D.C.: National Academy of Sciences-National Research Council, 1962.

————. *The WASHO Road Test, Part 2: Test Data, Analyses, Findings.* Special Report 22. Washington, D.C.: National Academy of Sciences-National Research Council, 1955.

Jorgensen, Roy et al. *Oversize-Overweight Permit Operation on State Highways.* National Cooperative Highway Research Program Report 80. Washington, D.C.: National Academy of Sciences, National Academy of Engineering, 1969.

Kent, Malcolm F. "The Freight's the Weight." *Proceedings of the Thirty-Seventh Annual Meeting of the Highway Research Board, January 6–10, 1958.* Washington, D.C.: National Academy of Sciences, National Research Council, 1958.

Stevens, Hoy. *Line-Haul Trucking Costs in Relation to Vehicle Gross Weights.* Highway Research Board. Bulletin 301. Washington, D.C.: National Academy of Sciences, National Research Council, 1961.

————. "Line-Haul Trucking Costs Upgraded, 1964." Highway Research Record, no. 127. Washington, D.C.: Highway Research Board, 1966.

Whiteside, Robert E. et al. *Changes in Legal Vehicle Weights and Dimensions: Some Economic Effects on Highways.* National Cooperative Highway Research Program Report 141. Washington, D.C.: Highway Research Board, National Research Council, National Academy of Sciences, National Academy of Engineering, 1973.

Books

American Association of State Highway Officials. *Policy on Maximum Dimensions and Weights of Motor Vehicles to be Operated Over the Highways of the United States.* N.p., 1963.

American Trucking Trends 1974. Washington, D.C.: American Trucking Associations, 1974.

Case, Leland S., and Lester B. Lave. "Inland Waterway Transportation: Some Evidence on Cost."
   In *Criteria for Transport Pricing,* eds. Marvin L. Fair and James R. Nelson. Cambridge,
   Md.: Cornell Maritime Press, 1973.

Crawford, F. G. *Motor Fuel Taxation in the United States.* Baltimore: Lord Baltimore Press, 1939.

———. *The Administration of the Gasoline Tax in the United States.* 3rd ed. New York: Municipal
   Administration Service, 1932.

———. *The Gasoline Tax in the United States.* Chicago: Public Administration Service, 1936.

Davis, Grant M. *Transportation Regulation: A Pragmatic Assessment.* Danville, Ill.: Interstate
   Publishers, 1976.

———. *The Department of Transportation.* Lexington, Mass.: D. C. Heath, 1974.

Davis, Grant M., and Stephen W. Brown. *Logistics Management.* Lexington, Mass.: D. C. Heath,
   1975.

Davis, Grant M., Martin T. Farris, and Jack J. Holder, Jr. *Management of Transportation
   Carriers.* New York: Praeger, 1975.

Grubbs, Edward C. *A Review of Literature Pertaining to the Development, Subsequent Evaluations
   and Current Use of the General AASHO Road Test Equation.* Technical Report No. 1,
   Highway Research Project No. 20, Arkansas State Highway Department Planning and
   Research Division. Fayetteville, Ark.: University of Arkansas, 1965.

Johnson, A. E., ed. *AASHO—The First Fifty Years—1914–1964.* Washington, D.C.: American
   Association of State Highway Officials, 1965.

Learned, Edmund P. *State Gasoline Taxes.* Bulletin of the University of Kansas Humanistic
   Studies 26, no. 6. Lawrence, Kans.: University of Kansas, 1925.

McMillan, Claude, and Richard F. Gonzalez. *Systems Analysis: A Computer Approach to Decision
   Models.* Homewood, Ill.: Richard D. Irwin, 1968.

Meier, Robert C.; William T. Newell; and Harold L. Pazer. *Simulation in Business and Economics.*
   Englewood Cliffs, N.J.: Prentice-Hall, 1969.

1975 Motor Truck Facts. New York: Motor Vehicle Manufacturers Association of the United
   States, 1975.

Owen, Wilfred. *A Study in Highway Economics.* Cambridge, Mass.: Alpha Chapter of Massachusetts, Phi Beta Kappa, 1934.

Salmon, Armand J., Jr. et al. *Financing Highways.* Princeton: Tax Institute, 1957.

Taff, Charles A. *Commercial Motor Transportation.* 3rd ed. Homewood, Ill.: Richard D. Irwin,
   1961.

Transportation Association of America. *Transportation Facts and Trends,* 11th ed. Washington,
   D.C.: Transportation Association of America, December 1974.

————. *Transportation Facts and Trends,* 11th ed. Washington, D.C.: Transportation Association of America, October 1975.

Trull, Edna. *Borrowing for Highways.* New York: Dun and Bradstreet, 1937.

Western Highway Institute. *State Motor Carriers Handbook: Sizes and Weights, Taxes and Fees.* Chicago: Commerce Clearing House, 1975.

Wilson, George W. *Essays on Some Unsettled Questions in the Economics of Transportation.* Bloomington, Ind.: Indiana University, Foundation for Economic and Business Studies, 1962.

Periodicals

Abel, I. W. " 'Suddenly' There's an Energy Crisis." *Viewpoint* 3 (Fourth Quarter, 1973): 1.

American Trucking Associations. "The Case for Twin Trailers." 4th ed. (1974), pp. 1–8.

————. "Typical Present Tractor, Dolly, and Trailer Weights and Dimensions." Mimeographed N.d.

Carnes, Richard B. "Productivity Trends in Intercity Trucking." *Monthly Labor Review* 97 (January 1974): 53–57.

Collymore, Walter A. "Computer Technology: A Key to Improved Productivity in Transportation.' *Traffic World* 162 (June 23, 1975): 35–37.

Diacoff, Darwin W. "Analyzing 'Productivity Trends in Intercity Trucking.'" *Monthly Labor Review* 97 (October 1974): 41–45.

Davis, Grant M. "Federal Highway Safety Programs—Organizational Disunity." *Journal of the Alabama Academy of Science* 42 (January 1971): 54–63.

————. "One Way to Improve Trucking Safety." *The Arizona Roadrunner* 22, no. 4 (April 1969): 6–8.

————. "Proposed Federal Changes in Interstate Highway Route Selection and Design." *Alabama Business* 39 (May 15, 1969): 1–3.

Davis, Grant M., and Martin T. Farris. "Federal Transportation Safety Programs—Misdirected Emphasis and Wasted Resources." *Transportation Journal* 2, no. 4 (Summer 1972): 5–17.

————. "The Transportation Paradox and the Federal Research and Development Function." *ICC Practitioners' Journal* 39 (May–June 1972): 513–24.

Davis, Grant M., and Phillip H. Taylor. "Impact of Fuel Shortages on Arkansas: A Preliminary Evaluation." *Arkansas Business and Economic Review* 6 (May 1973): 28–35.

"FHWA Studies Truck Size-Weight Move to Conserve Fuel, Increase Productivity." *Traffic World* 157 (February 4, 1974): 19–20.

Flott, Allan C.; Lana R. Batts; and Ronald D. Roth. "The Ton-Mile, Does It Properly Measure Transportation Output?" Presentation to the Transportation Research Board, Commission on Societal Technologies, National Research Council. Washington, D.C.: Department of Research and Transport Economics, American Trucking Associations, 1975.

"House and Senate Approve Federal-Aid Highway Bill, Raise Truck Weight Limits." *Traffic World* 160 (December 23, 1974): 9.

Kadanoff, Leo P. "From Simulation to Public Policy: An Examination of Forrester's 'Urban Dynamics' " *Simulation* 16 (June 1971): 261–68.

Karr, Albert R. "Whoosh! Here Come the Big Rigs." *Wall Street Journal,* December 17, 1974, p. 14.

McLeod, John. "Simulation Today—From Fuzz to Fact." *Simulation* 20 (March 1973): 9–12.

Quast, Theodore. "The Output Unit in Transportation." *Transportation Journal* 10 (Winter 1970): 5–7.

Ringham, Rodger F. " 'Reguflation'—The Trauma of Truck Transport." *Traffic World* 162 (June 23, 1975): 51–55.

Rinquest, Randall A. "Current Legal Problems in the Motor Fuel Tax Field." *North American Gasoline Tax Conference, Forty-Third Annual Report.* Concord: Evans Printing Company, 1969.

Rosenberg, Jess N. "Motor Carrier Comments." *North American Gasoline Tax Conference, Twenty-Eighth Annual Report.* Concord: Evans Printing Company, 1954.

————. "Trucking Views on Highway Tax Equities." *North American Gasoline Tax Conference, Thirty-Seventh Annual Report.* Concord: Evans Printing Company, 1963.

Staley, Richard A.; John L. Reith; and E. V. Kiley. "American Trucking and the Energy Crisis." Department of Research and Transport Economics, American Trucking Associations, April 1973.

"State Legal Maximum Dimensions and Weights of Motor Vehicles Compared with AASHTO Standards." Prepared by the American Association of State Highway and Transportation Officials, December 31, 1974.

"State Legal Maximum Dimensions and Weights of Motor Vehicles Compared with AASHTO Standards." Prepared by the American Association of State Highway and Transport Officials, December 31, 1975.

Strauch, Patricia G. "Modeling in the Social Sciences: An Approach to Good Theory and Good Policy." *Simulation* 26 (January 1976): 153–56.

"Truck Taxes by State." 24th Annual Edition. Department of Research and Transport Economics, American Trucking Associations, 1975.

"Truck Weight Increase Vetoed." *Traffic Topics.* September-October, 1974, p. 14.

Western Highway Institute. "Effects of the Federal-Aid Highway Amendments of 1974 on State Axle and Gross Weight Limits as of November 1, 1975." Research Summary Series, no. 1-75 (October 17, 1975).

"What Is the Status of Truck Size-Weights?" *Traffic World* 165 (February 16, 1976): 36–40.

"What Shippers Should Know About Truck Size and Weight Limits." *Traffic World* 154 (June 25, 1973): 33–37.

Proceedings

Proceedings of the Interstate Commerce Commission's Productivity Measurement Conference on November 26, 1974. Washington, D.C.: Government Printing Office, 1975.

GRANT M. DAVIS was born on May 26, 1937, in Tuscaloosa, Alabama, and educated in Atlanta, Georgia. He is currently the Oren Harris Professor of Transportation and a member of the Graduate Faculty in the University of Arkansas' College of Business Administration. Dr. Davis has considerable industrial experience with Ford Motor Company and the Mason and Dixon Lines in the fields of traffic, transportation, and distribution. He has authored more than 80 major journal and technical articles in such publications as *ICC Practitioners' Journal, Transportation Journal, Traffic Quarterly, Quarterly Review of Economics and Business,* and *The Logistics Review.* He is the author of *The Department of Transportation* (Lexington, Mass.: D. C. Heath, 1970); *Logistics Management* (Lexington, Mass.: D. C. Heath, 1974); *Rate Bureau and Antitrust Conflicts* (New York: Praeger, 1975); and *Management of Transportation Carriers* (New York: Praeger, 1975). Dr. Davis has extensive consulting experience in the areas of business and government. He is an Interstate Commerce Commission Practitioner and a member of the Association of Interstate Commerce Commission's Bar, American Society of Traffic and Transportation, Delta Nu Alpha, Society of Logistics Engineers, American Economics Association, Southern Marketing Association, Beta Gamma Sigma, and the Alabama Academy of Science. He was named National Transportation Man-of-the-Year in 1971 by Delta Nu Alpha and is listed in Outstanding Educators in America, Who's Who in the West, Personalities of the South, International Biography, Who's Who in the Southwest, and Contemporary Authors of America.

JOHN E. DILLARD, JR., is Assistant Professor of Marketing, College of Business, Department of Business Administration, the Virginia Polytechnic Institute and State University, Blacksburg, Virginia. Dr. Dillard received his Ph.D. in Business Administration from the University of Arkansas in 1976, his M.S. in Management from the University of Arkansas in 1973, and his B.A. in English from Wilmington College in 1968. He has written numerous articles that have appeared in such publications as the *Transportation Journal* and *Traffic Quarterly.*

*COST-BENEFIT ANALYSIS, new and expanded edition
E. J. Mishan

THE ENERGY CRISIS AND THE ENVIRONMENT
edited by Donald R. Kelley

ENVIRONMENTAL LEGISLATION: A Sourcebook
edited by Mary Robinson Sive

MANAGEMENT OF TRANSPORTATION CARRIERS
Grant M. Davis
Martin T. Farris
Jack J. Holder, Jr.

RATE BUREAUS AND ANTITRUST CONFLICTS IN
TRANSPORTATION: Public Policy Issues
Grant M. Davis
Charles S. Sherwood

*Also available in paperback as a PSS Student Edition